Big-Print Quilts

75

Karen Snyder

©2008 Karen Snyder

Published by

kp **krause publications**
An Imprint of F+W Publications

700 East State Street • Iola, WI 54990-0001
715-445-2214 • 888-457-2873
www.krausebooks.com

Our toll-free number to place an order or obtain
a free catalog is (800) 258-0929.

Library of Congress Control Number: 2006935763
ISBN-13: 978-0-89689-481-5
ISBN-10: 0-89689-481-9

Designed by Rachael Knier
Edited by Andy Belmas
Printed in China

Dedication

This book is dedicated to all those wonderful fabric designers who keep inspiring us with their creativity and challenging us to create new quilts.

Acknowledgments

I would like to thank the many wonderful people who helped make this book possible.

*Darlene Zimmerman for being my mentor.

*Candy Wiza for always listening to my ideas.

*Andy Belmas for his editing skills.

*Rachael Knier for her graphic design and persistence in getting everything right.

*My parents for teaching by example.

*The women who so willingly made quilts for the book: Connie Nason, Cortné Stricker, Monica Solorio-Snow, Pat Hall, Beverly Wakeman, Carol Osterholm, and Sue Fair.

*A second and special thanks to my girl gang: Connie Nason, Monica-Solorio Snow, and Cortné Stricker for coming to my aid over and over again.

*My husband, Bob Hamilton, and the rest of my family for believing in me.

*Elna USA for the opportunity to sew on the fine 7300 Pro Quilting Queen.

Contents

6 Introduction

10 General Instructions

16 PROJECTS

16 The Big Shake

24 The Little Shake
   Table Runner

28 The Great Gatsby

34 Grand Daddy

40 Hercules

48 Big Sky

54 Big Thunder

60 Grandeur

64 Picture Window

70 Whopper

76 Grand Prix

82 Frame-Up Table Runner

86 Grand Canyon

94 Big Bertha

104 Feature Presentation

110 Resources
111 About the Author

Introduction

How many times have you been browsing through the quilt shop and been enchanted by a big, beautiful print. You look at that fabric for the longest time, falling more and more in love with it, but then you walk away. You ask yourself, "How would I ever be able to use something with that large scale in a quilt?"

This book was written just to answer that question. There are lots of ways to use those big prints—and not just for borders or backs. Here you'll find ideas for cutting them up into small pieces, leaving them as big pieces and working them into many different, beautiful quilts.

Besides the large floral prints, Asian prints, paisleys, and toiles, there's another whole category—novelty prints. These are plentiful in the marketplace. Some are whimsical, almost cartoonish. Others are thematic, cowboys or hot rods for instance. There are also lots of novelty prints perfect for children's quilts, like robots, paper dolls, and fairy tale characters. These, too, can present a challenge for the quilter—until now. Turn the pages of this book and imagine your favorite giant poppy print or puppy dog fabric in one of these quilts. Hopefully you won't walk away from big prints next time one catches your fancy.

Working with Big Prints

Not all big prints are created equal. Designs may be directional or tossed, tightly packed or separated by lots of background. Each of these qualities needs to be considered when choosing a fabric and pattern. Each can present its own set of challenges, but none should be overlooked. Just be aware of the unique properties of each type of print and work with them rather than fight them.

When looking at the patterns in the book, don't limit yourself to using fabrics that look "just like the photo." Fabrics come and go quickly in today's market and chances are you won't find the exact fabrics featured in the projects. You may want to find something similar, but keep an open mind when looking at the patterns. Where I've used a floral print, you may want to substitute a toile. A quilt in which I've used a novelty print may be perfect for that Asian-inspired piece you've been saving.

Often when working with big prints you may need extra fabric so you can do some fussy cutting. Fussy cutting is nothing more than centering an element of the design in the patches or strips you are cutting. To some it may seem wasteful to fussy cut as you often have odd pieces of fabric left over. But hey, we're quilters. We know what to do with left over pieces of fabric—save them for another project. There's really no such thing as wasted fabric to the true quilter.

SCATTERED PRINTS

Some big prints are scattered across the fabric with a lot of background showing. This is not a bad thing, but should be considered when choosing which quilts to make from them. Generally it is better to choose a quilt pattern that doesn't require cutting the big-print fabric into lots of small pieces. If there is strong contrast between the design and the background color, the edges of your piecing may become lost. Fussy cutting or using large pieces of a scattered design will result in a more successful quilt.

PACKED PRINTS

Packed designs are just that—prints that have the pattern packed closely together without a lot of background showing. Even though they are large scale, prints of this type lend themselves well to cutting into smaller pieces and don't need to be fussy cut.

DIRECTIONAL PRINTS

Directional prints can be handled two ways. You can ignore the directionality of the print, and let pieces lay in every direction in the quilt. This is not a bad approach and the results can be lovely. If you decide to do this, you'll want to take a few minutes when laying out the blocks to be sure that the design does, indeed, go in all directions. If 80% of the design is going in the same direction, the 20% that is different looks out of place. However, if the directional print is turned equally throughout the quilt the pattern will look balanced.

You may prefer to keep the integrity of the design intact by making sure the direction of the print is the same throughout the quilt. Planning must start before cutting the fabric for the desired effect to be achieved. You will also want to be sure that you have enough fabric, especially if you are using it in the borders. Two of the borders will need to be cut lengthwise and two will need to be cut crosswise.

Scattered prints often have a lot of background showing.

Packed prints have the elements of the print packed closely together.

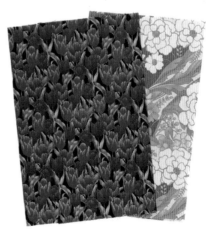

Directional prints may take extra planning before cutting.

Novelty prints can reflect a person's interest or hobbies.

Opportunity cloth can be cut up and used in pieced quilts with interesting results.

NOVELTY PRINTS

Novelty prints have been around for centuries and come in many scales. It wasn't uncommon to see small dogs or horseshoes on shirting prints from the late 1800's or toys and children in a small scale on prints from the 1920's and 30's. In recent years, however, novelty prints have exploded, both in the size of the prints and the number of offerings from which to choose. You can find novelty prints that reflect your favorite movie and cartoon characters, hobbies such as bull riding or fishing, trendy themes like fashion or tattoos, favorite foods and even pin-up guys and gals. These novelty prints make up into wonderful gift quilts that reflect the recipient's taste.

OPPORTUNITY CLOTH

While not as plentiful as novelty prints, there are often opportunity fabrics available. These are sometimes referred to as "cheater cloth."

The designs may look like a patchwork or appliqué quilt but are printed on the fabric. They are usually meant to be used just as they are, without being cut. However, when you come across prints of this type, consider how they might look if cut up and used in another way.

Beyond Big Prints

The quilts in this book often have large, uncut areas in the patchwork blocks. This helps feature the big prints. It also creates an opportunity for using something other than big prints in these patterns. Consider embroidery blocks, appliqué blocks, photo transfers, sampler blocks, and T-shirts.

EMBROIDERED BLOCKS

Whether they are vintage, hand-stitched blocks or designs created with today's computer-aided embroidery machines, embroidered blocks deserve to be shown to their best advantage when used in a quilt. Rather than just adding sashing between the blocks, you might try inserting them into some patterns featured here. Large blocks could take center stage in Hercules and smaller squares could be shown off by using them in every other round of The Great Gatsby.

APPLIQUÉ BLOCKS

Appliqué blocks can be simply fused and stitched around with a zigzag or buttonhole stitch, or they may be patiently hand turned and affixed to a background with tiny stitches. No matter how you do your appliqué, those blocks deserve to be featured prominently in a quilt and shown to their best advantage. Blocks appliquéd on-point could be featured in Big Sky. For a setting that looks like it's on-point but isn't, try Big Bertha.

PHOTO TRANSFERS

It is easy to transfer photos to fabric. Make a memory quilt with treasured photos from a family gathering, a family tree quilt with photos of your parents and grandparents or commemorate a special family vacation with the snapshots your brought home. If your photos are different sizes, take a cue from the quilt called Whopper and frame the photos with small squares. You may even want to coordinate your fabrics with the theme of your quilt. If you have just a few special photos, Feature Presentation would be a lovely way to showcase them.

T-SHIRTS

T-shirt quilts can be a fun way to turn memories into something enduring. For ten years I traveled to different Lewis and Clark events. I often bought T-shirts to commemorate the different destinations. Now that the Lewis and Clark bicentennial is history, I plan to turn those T-shirts into a special quilt using the Picture Windows or Grand Prix pattern. To make a T-shirt quilt, just add a stabilizer to the back of the T-shirt fabric, fussy cut the design and continue as you would for any other quilt.

Settings

Blocks can be put together with a variety of settings. The quilts in this book are grouped into four categories:

SIDE BY SIDE

Very simply, blocks set this way are sewn together one to another. Although this is a simple setting, blocks that are set side by side can create great impact.

SIMPLY SASHED

Sashing strips separate blocks in a quilt. The sashing may be fabric strips or made up of pieced elements like flying geese.

FRAMED

Just like frames on pictures, frames on fabric can be a great way to draw attention to a big print. Frames can be straight, twisted or just on two sides of a block.

ALTERNATE BLOCK

An alternate block can help form a secondary pattern. This pattern then helps frame the focus of the big print.

General Instruction

Four Keys to Success

There are four basic things that you need to master to become a successful quilter:

1. Accurate cutting
2. A ¼" seam allowance
3. Good pressing techniques
4. Measuring through the middle when adding your borders

Of course, you still need to quilt and bind your project, but if you pay attention to these four principles, your seams will match and your quilt top will lay flat.

CUTTING

Accurate cutting is the first step in making quilts that go together easily and lay flat. Proper tools make cutting easy. Be sure that your rotary cutter has a sharp blade with no nicks, that you have a ruler that is at least 24" long and that your mat is free of grooves.

The most common problem when cutting is letting the ruler wiggle as you make your cut. To avoid this, spread your fingers apart and place the fingertips on the half of the ruler that is closest to you. Do not lay your palm flat on the ruler. Place your rotary cutter next to ruler and cut about half way across your fabric. Leaving your cutter in place, walk the fingers of the hand that is on the ruler up to the half of the ruler that is farthest from you. Press downward with your fingertips and continue making the cut.

Get familiar with your cutting tools and learn to read your ruler correctly. If you are cutting a lot of strips that are the same size, it can be helpful to put a narrow piece of masking tape on the back of the ruler at the proper measurement. That way you can quickly see that you are lining up properly.

Did you know that your index finger should be placed on the top of your rotary cutter? Every brand of rotary cutter has a place for your index finger. If you grip your cutter by wrapping your fingers around the handle, your wrist is twisted and your hand is in an awkward position. By placing your index finger on the top of your cutter, you have a straight line from your elbow. This is ergonomically correct and won't lead to problems with your wrist or elbow.

SEAM ALLOWANCE

Once you've cut your pieces accurately, it is important to sew them together using a ¼" seam. Many sewing machines come with a ¼" foot, or a special ¼" foot can be purchased for them. If you do a lot of quilting, you may want to consider this. If you do not have a ¼" foot, lay your acrylic ruler under your needle. Slowly, by hand, lower your needle until it just rests on the ¼" mark. Use a piece of masking tape on your machine to mark along the edge of ruler. Use this tape as a guide when sewing your seams.

To make sure that you are using your ¼" foot correctly, or that you have your masking tape in the correct position, do this experiment. Cut two 2" strips of fabric, about 3" long. Lay the strips together and sew along the long side with a ¼" seam. Press. Now use your ruler to measure the width of the piece. It should be 3½". If not, make adjustments and repeat the experiment.

PRESSING

Pressing is just what is says—pressing. You want to press your fabrics and your seams without distorting them. It requires a gentle touch to do this. Whether or not to use steam is a matter of personal preference, but be aware that you are more likely to distort your fabrics if you are using steam.

When quilting, seams are generally pressed to one side as opposed to being pressed open. When pressing seams to one side, it is very important to press *from the front.* Lay the pieced patches on the ironing board. Since you will usually want to press your seam toward the darker fabric, lay the pieced patch with the darker fabric on the top. This will automatically make the seam allowance lay toward the darker fabric when you separate the patches. Before opening, give the seam a quick press to help marry the sewing threads to the fabric. Then gently lift the top layer of fabric. Use the side of the iron to lay it over and press. By pressing from the front in this manner, you will avoid leaving little folds or pleats at the seams. These little pleats can have an adverse effect when you join your blocks or rows together.

BORDERS

Borders on a quilt act like a frame on a picture—they serve to contain the action going on in the body of the work. Often this can be accomplished with a narrow border of an accent fabric and a wider border that matches the tone and value of the blocks. You can also use borders to increase the size of finished quilt. Each of the projects in the book gives you suggestions for choosing appropriate borders.

While borders may be the finishing touch to your masterpiece, if applied incorrectly, they can cause problems. If you merely cut a long strip and start sewing it to the edges of your quilt top, the border strip has a tendency to "grow," and the quilt won't lay flat. This occurs because the edges of your quilt include numerous seams which can become "unlocked" when you handle the quilt top. As you add the border to the edge of top, each seam may open a little, causing the problem.

You can, however, create a quilt top that lays flat every time. It's as simple as measuring correctly and cutting the border strips the proper length before adding them.

After piecing and assembling the quilt blocks, find a flat surface on which to lay the finished top. Using a tape measure, measure the length of the quilt *through the middle.* Cut two strips of border fabric this length. Find the center of the strip and the center of the quilt top. This can be done by folding the fabric in half and finger pressing. Pin the border strip to the quilt top at the center point. Next, pin the top and bottom edge. Continue pinning every few inches, easing if necessary. Sew the seam with a ¼ seam allowance. Press toward the border fabric.

Next, you will want to measure the width of the quilt top. Again, measure *through the middle.* This is what will assure that your finished top will lay flat. Cut two strips of border fabric this length. Find the centers, pin, stitch and press. If there are multiple borders, repeat the steps, doing the lengthwise borders first.

PREWASHING FABRICS

To wash or not to wash—that is the question. If you buy good, quality cotton fabric, prewashing is not a necessity. I prefer not to wash my fabrics for a couple of reasons. First, I like the crispness of unwashed fabric. If you wash your fabrics, you remove the sizing. Secondly, I don't always have time. Often when I get new fabrics, I just can't wait to cut into them! If I take the time to prewash, the inspiration may be gone. Lastly, I like the look you get when you wash a finished quilt and it puckers up just a bit around your quilting stitches.

If you choose to prewash, don't just toss the fabric into the washer and dryer. You risk losing too much fabric due to frayed edges. Shrinkage is minimal with good quality cotton fabrics. The main reason for prewashing is to remove any excess dye. You can do this easily without sending your fabrics for a spin in the washer and a tumble in the dryer. Follow these guidelines for prewashing:

1   Fill your sink or a basin with tepid water. Put your fabrics into the water and swish them around. If you notice a lot of dye being released, change the water and repeat until the water stays clear.

2   Place each fabric on a towel. Roll the towel around it and squeeze gently, then drape it on anything handy until it is nearly dry.

3   When the fabrics are still damp, press them with a dry iron until they are completely dry. If you wait too long, and the fabrics are completely dry, just spray them with a mist of water, wait a few minutes, then press.

4   You may want to use some spray sizing on your fabrics once you have pressed them dry. The sizing will give your fabrics body and make them easier to cut and stitch.

BATTINGS

There are many choices of batting to use in your quilt. Batting can be made from natural fibers like cotton, wool, or even silk. They can also be made from polyester or a combination of a natural fiber and polyester. As well, there are different weights, thickness and lofts to consider. I mostly use cotton blends as I like the flat look and ease of care that they provide. Occasionally I use a polyester bat, but look for one that drapes well and doesn't have too much loft.

LAYERING AND BASTING

Once your quilt top is complete, you will need to make a quilt "sandwich" before you begin quilting. The quilt sandwich is made up of the quilt back, batting and the pieced top. The backing and batting should be at least 4" larger than the quilt top.

1   After doing any necessary piecing of the backing fabric, tape the fabric, wrong side up, to a flat surface. Take care to insure that the fabric is pulled taut.

2   Lay the batting over the backing and smooth out any wrinkles.

3   Lay the well-pressed quilt top, right side up, on top of the batting.

4   If you will be hand quilting, baste with long running stitches. If you will be machine quilting, baste with safety pins.

Quilting

There are so many choices for quilting today. Traditional hand quilting, quilting on your home sewing machine, midarm and longarm quilting machines, even computerized quilting machines.

While I have a longarm and do my large quilts on it, I prefer a regular sewing machine for smaller items like table runners and wall hangings. Many people prefer to take their finished quilt tops to a professional to be quilted.

All of the quilts in the book have suggestions for finishing. These are just suggestions and you should feel free to experiment and put your own finishing touch on your projects.

The fabric and pattern you've chosen have set the tone for your finished quilt. The quilting can enhance or detract from your finished project, so spend some time deciding how you're going to quilt it.

Thread color can make or break your quilting. When you have a pattern that has lots of contrast between the fabrics, consider using two different colors of thread for the quilting. I often quilt the dark areas of a quilt with dark thread, then go back and quilt the lighter areas with a matching light thread. Occasionally I'll leave small elements unquilted. This will allow those elements to stand out a bit.

Binding

1. Cut binding strips 2¼" wide.

2. After cutting the required number of strips, piece them together with diagonal seams.

3. Press seams open.

4. Press the binding in half lengthwise, wrong sides together.

5. Trim excess batting and backing from quilted top.

6. Beginning in the middle of the quilt, place the folded binding strip right sides together along the edge of the quilt. The raw edges of the binding and the raw edges of the quilt should be together. Pin one side.

7. Beginning six or seven inches from the end of the binding strip, stitch with a ¼" seam. Stop stitching ¼" from the corner.

8. Backstitch.

9. Pivot the quilt. Fold the binding strip up at a 45-degree angle then back down.

10. Begin sewing at the top edge of the quilt.

11. Continue around all four corners. Stop stitching approximately 6 inches from the beginning of the strip. This will leave about 12" of binding unsewn.

12. In the middle of this space, fold back the loose ends of the strips so they meet.

13. Mark a dot along the fold at this point.

14. Open the binding strips.

15. Pivot, aligning the dots, and sew the strips together with a diagonal seam.

16. Trim excess binding and attach the unsewn area to quilt.

17. Fold the binding over the raw edge of the quilt so that it covers the machine stitching on the backside.

18. Stitch in place using a blind stitch. A miter will form at the corners of your quilt.

Labeling

I can't stress enough how important it is to label your quilts. Have you ever had the frustration of looking through old family photograph albums and wondering about the ancestors who stare out at your from faded photographs? I feel the same way when I look at antique and vintage quilts.

Quilts have a story to tell. Even unlabeled quilts tell a story. The fabrics used in them are a clue to their age. The precision of the stitching is an indication of the maker's skill. The amount of wear tells whether the quilt was used as a utility quilt or made for display. Missing is the who, what, when and where. Who made the quilt, what was the occasion, when was it made and where did the quilt maker live? A simple label stitched to the back of a quilt can answer all of these questions.

Quilt labels can be simple or elaborate. A piece of muslin with the pertinent information written in permanent ink and whip stitched to the back of the quilt will suffice. If you are feeling more creative, you can embroider a label by hand or machine and embellish it with additional needlework. Photos transferred to fabric add a personal touch to a quilt. Decorative fabric labels are also available. These often have a floral design around the border and a blank area for you to add your personal information.

My favorite way to make a label is:

1. Type the information you want into a word processing program on your computer. Use font and type sizes that are easy to read. A 16 to 24 point type size is ideal.

2. Print the information and tape the paper to a desk or table.

3. Tape an unwashed piece of muslin over the paper.

4. Using a fine-point permanent pen, trace over the letters.

5. Remove the tape. Press edges under ¼".

6. Stitch the label to the back of the quilt.

Future generations will thank you!

Labels can be as plain or fancy as you wish.

Special Techniques

Pre-printed papers are available that have a grid drawn on them that allows you to make multiple half-square triangles at a time. This method is both quick and accurate. I highly recommend these papers. They are usually printed on newsprint and are easy to remove.

You can also make your own triangle papers by drawing a grid onto paper. Newsprint works best as it's easy to remove after you've stitched through it. Copier paper also works well.

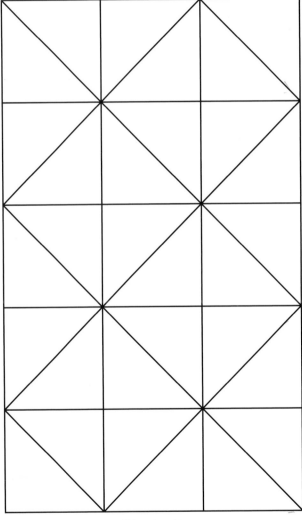

Triangle grid.

To make 2 finished half-square triangles:

1. Cut a piece of lightweight paper 9" x 15". Draw $2\frac{7}{8}$" squares on the paper, three across and five down. Draw diagonal lines through all the squares.

2. Place the two fabrics for the half-square triangles right sides together. Pin the paper securely to the fabric. Stitch a ¼" from both sides of the diagonal lines. Use a short stitch length to make paper removal easier.

3. Press. Cut apart on all the drawn lines, both straight and diagonal. Remove the paper and press the half-square triangles open. One paper will yield 30 half-square triangles!

The Big Shake

The fractured look of this quilt is easy to achieve with a few slices of a rotary cutter and a ¼" seam. The uncut border calms the overall look.

Pieced by Connie Nason and the author, quilted by the author.

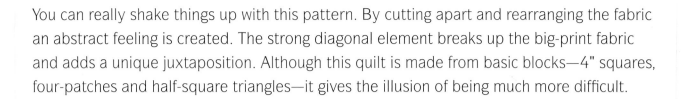

You can really shake things up with this pattern. By cutting apart and rearranging the fabric an abstract feeling is created. The strong diagonal element breaks up the big-print fabric and adds a unique juxtaposition. Although this quilt is made from basic blocks—4" squares, four-patches and half-square triangles—it gives the illusion of being much more difficult.

Measurements

Quilt: 96" x 112"
Block: 4"

Fabric Requirements

- 7½ yd. big-print fabric for 4" blocks and half-square triangles—more if fussy cutting
- 1 yd. red accent fabric for 4" blocks
- 2¾ yd. navy fabric for four-patches, half-square triangles and binding
- ⅝ yd. yellow fabric for four-patches
- 8½ yd. backing fabric
- 100" x 116" batting

Choosing Fabric

This is a great way to showcase a novelty print like the one shown here. Look for a design with strong elements and good contrast, rather than one with a blended look. Whether you choose a floral or novelty fabric, the design elements can be quite large and you'll still have success with this quilt. When working with a multi-colored print, it's easy to draw upon the colors present for the accent fabrics. Small-scale prints, solids or fabrics that read as a solid work well for the accent blocks. **Consider making this quilt using the following types of fabric: scattered prints, directional prints or novelty prints.**

What are fabrics that "read as solid?" Fabrics that are tone-on-tone prints that don't have much variation in value. Every fabric company has its own version of a dimpled, tone-on-tone or subtle blender print available. Stepping back from these fabrics, the pattern shouldn't be obvious, it should look like a solid color.

Cutting Instructions

Note: All strips are cut across the width of the fabric.

FROM THE BIG-PRINT FABRIC, CUT:

10 6½" strips for the border.

Note: If the print in your big-print fabric is directional, you will want to cut enough strips lengthwise for two of your borders.

38 4½" strips. Sub cut into **342** 4½" squares.

You can shake the design up a bit more when sub cutting your strips into squares. Simply shift some of the strips to the right or left slightly so the pattern doesn't line up just the way it was printed when you sew the squares back together.

5 4⅞" strips. Sub cut into **39** 4⅞" squares.

FROM THE RED FABRIC, CUT:

7 4½" strips. Sub cut into **56** 4½" squares.

FROM THE NAVY FABRIC, CUT:

5 4⅞" strips. Sub cut into **39** 4⅞" squares.
5 2½" strips for four-patches.
9 2½" strips for the inner border.
10 2¼" strips for binding.

FROM THE YELLOW FABRIC, CUT:

5 2½" strips for four-patches.
1 6½" strip for border corners. Sub cut into **4** 6½" squares, and **4** 2½" squares.

Piecing the Blocks

FOUR-PATCHES

1   Join one 2½" strip of navy fabric, right sides together, with one 2½" strip of yellow fabric. Press toward the navy fabric. Repeat to make five strip sets. Press toward the navy.

2   Cut each strip set into 2½" segments. Join two segments to make a four-patch as shown in Figure 1. Make 40 four-patches.

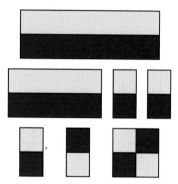

Fig. 1. Four-patches. Make 40.

HALF-SQUARE TRIANGLES

3   Draw a diagonal line on the wrong side of 39 navy 4⅞" squares. Place a navy fabric onto a 4⅞" square of big-print fabric with right sides together. The diagonal line should go from the upper left corner to the lower right corner as shown in Figure 2.

Fig. 2.

4   Stitch a ¼" on either side of the diagonal line and cut on the drawn line as shown in Figure 3.

Fig. 3.

5   Press to the dark fabric. Make 78 half-square triangles as shown in Figure 4.

Fig. 4.

Assembling the Top

1 Working on a design wall or on the floor, lay out the 4½" squares, four-patches and half-square triangles as shown in the Assembly Diagram on page 21.

Be sure the accent fabric in the four-patches creates a diagonal line.

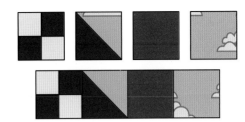

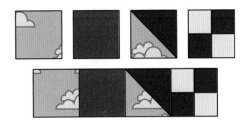

Fig. 5. Make 17.

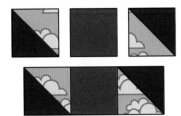

Fig. 6. Make 18.

Fig. 7. Make 17.

The Big Shake

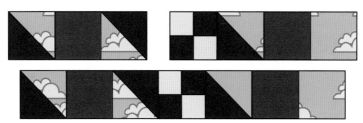

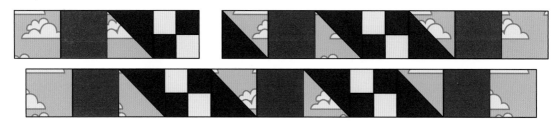

Fig. 8. Make 14.

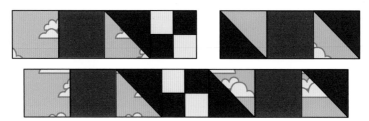

Fig. 9. Make 10

Fig. 10. Make 4.

Note: *Work with the focus fabric. You may want to keep the design elements together or arrange them in a way that visually breaks up the original image.*

2 Once you have the blocks laid out in a pleasing manner, join the blocks together in rows.

3 Press the block seams in each row in opposite directions. This will allow the seams in each row to nest with the seams in the row below it.

4 Join the rows together, working from the top down. Press.

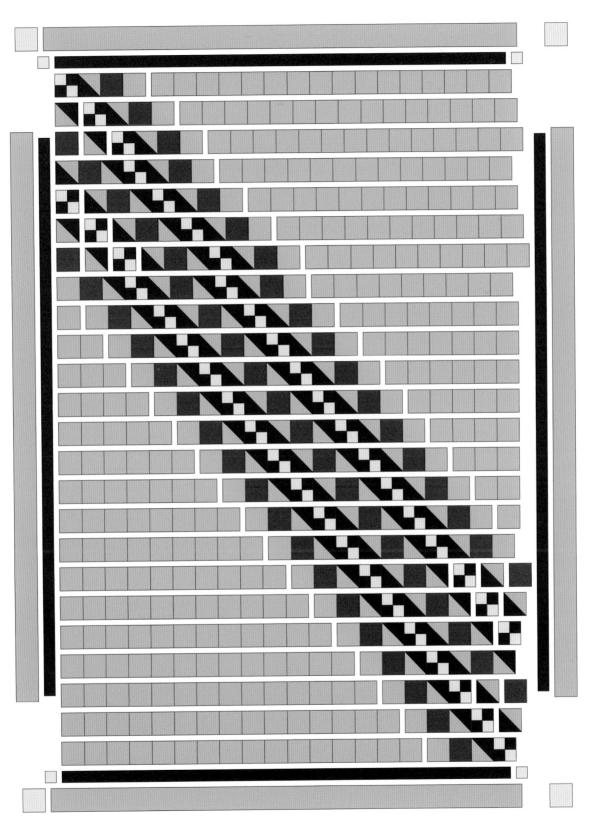

Assembly Diagram

Adding the Borders

INNER BORDER

1   Join the strips for the inner border together by sewing diagonal seams. Press open. Join all of the strips together until you have one long strip.

2   Measure the length of your quilt lengthwise *through the middle*. This will prevent you from having wavy borders. Mathematically this number would be 96½" but everyone's seam allowances vary, so be sure to measure.

3   Before adding borders to the side of the quilt, measure the top crosswise *through the middle*. This measurement should be 80½" but check your measurement to be sure. Cut two strips this length. Add a 2½" square of yellow fabric to each end of these strips.

4   Attach borders from Step 2 to each side of the quilt. Press. Attach borders from Step 3 to the top and bottom of the quilt. Press.

OUTER BORDER

1   Join the strips for the outer border together. Press seams open. Join all of the strips together until you have one long strip.

Note: If you cut the side borders from the length of the fabric, join them together and set aside before joining the top and bottom borders.

2   Measure the length of the quilt top lengthwise *through the middle*. This will prevent you from having wavy borders. Mathematically this number would be 100½" but everyone's seam allowances vary, so be sure to measure. Cut two strips this length.

3   Before adding borders to side of quilt, measure the top crosswise *through the middle*. This measurement should be 84½" but check your measurement to be sure. Cut two strips this length. Add a 6½" square of yellow fabric to each end of these strips.

4   Attach borders from Step 2 to each side of the quilt. Press. Attach borders from Step 3 to the top and bottom of the quilt. Press.

Finishing Your Quilt

1   Cut your backing fabric into three equal pieces. Join together.

2   Prepare your quilt sandwich following the Layering and Basting instructions on page 12.

3   The options for quilting this quilt are wide open. You may want to quilt in the ditch vertically and horizontally. An all-over design can be effective if it doesn't detract from the visual elements in the quilt.

4   Bind and label your quilt following the instructions on page 13.

The Little Shake Table Runner

*A fun big-print fabric and an accent are all it takes
to add pizzazz to an otherwise plain tabletop.*

Pieced and quilted by Sue Fair.

Have some fun with a scaled down and simplified version of The Big Shake quilt. In this table runner four-patches are all that's needed to shake things up—and dress up your table.

Measurements

Runner: 11½" x 40"
Block: 4"

Fabric Requirements

- ⅔ yd. big-print fabric
- ⅜ yd. accent fabric (includes binding)
- ⅜ yd. backing fabric
- 13" x 42" batting

Choosing Fabric

A busy leaf or floral print would work well in this runner. Because of the smaller overall size of a table runner a more compact design than used in the Big Shake would be appropriate here. While a floral print would bring a bit of color to your table, don't overlook the fun novelty prints with a kitchen twist that are available! *Consider making this quilt using the following types of fabric: scattered prints, packed prints or novelty prints.*

Cutting Instructions

Note: All strips are cut across the width of the fabric.

FROM THE BIG-PRINT FABRIC, CUT:

1. 7" strip. Sub cut into **3** 7" squares. Cut each square twice diagonally for side setting triangles.
2. 4½" strips. Sub cut into **12** 4½" squares.
2. 2½" strips for four-patches.

FROM THE ACCENT FABRIC, CUT:

2. 2½" strips for four-patches.
3. 2¼" strips for binding.

Piecing the Four-Patches

1. Join one 2½" strip of accent fabric, right sides together, with one 2½" strip of big-print fabric. Repeat to make two strip sets. Press toward the accent fabric.

2. Cut each strip set into 2½" segments. Join two segments to make a four-patch as shown in Figure 1. Make 12 four-patches.

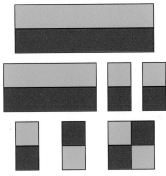

Fig. 1. Four-patch.

Assembling the Top

1 Assemble the units shown below. Press all seams away from the four-patches.

2 Once the units are pieced, lay them out as shown in the Assembly Diagram. Join rows together. Press.

Finishing Your Runner

1 Prepare your quilt sandwich following the Layering and Basting instructions on page 12. Quilting in the ditch is an easy and attractive finish for this runner. Bind following the instructions on page 13.

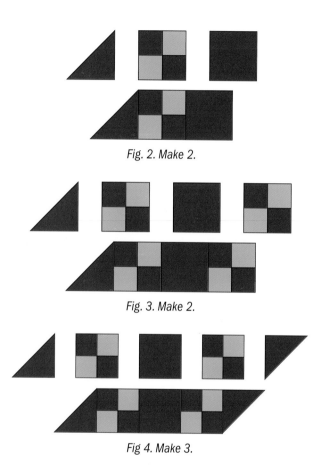

Fig. 2. Make 2.

Fig. 3. Make 2.

Fig 4. Make 3.

Assembly Diagram

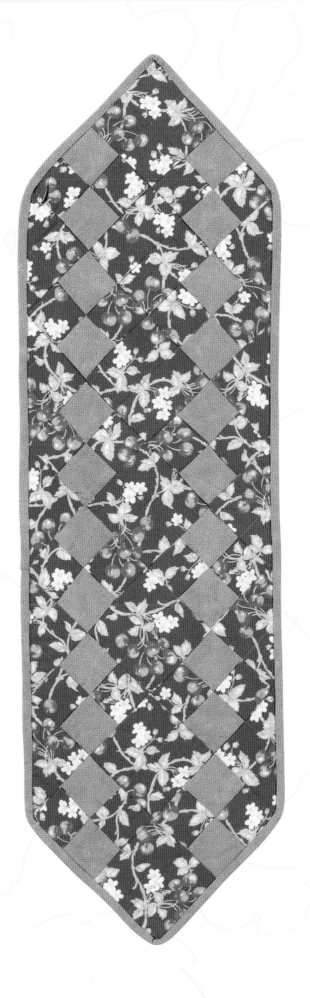

Great Gatsby

Just a touch of orange takes this quilt from average to eye-popping.

Pieced by Pat Hall and quilted by the author.

Here's a pattern that lets the beauty of the fabric, rather than intricate piecing, do the all the work. Combining a fabric with strong graphics, like this Jazz Age design, with some coordinating prints in a trip-around-the-world pattern results in a stunning quilt. With nothing but straight-line sewing you can create a king-sized masterpiece in a very short time. To allow for the possibility of needing to fussy cut the fabrics, this pattern is not strip pieced, but you'll find that the 6" squares sew up quickly. There will even be nine squares left over that work perfectly for a pieced pillow!

Measurements

Quilt: 106" x 118"
Block: 6"

Fabric Requirements

- 5 yd. black big-print fabric
- 2⅔ yd. white accent fabric #1
- 2 yd. blue accent fabric #2
- 2½ yd. orange accent fabric #3
- 9¼ yd. backing fabric
- 110" x 122" batting

Choosing Fabric

The simplicity of this design opens the door for creating a successful quilt from almost any style fabric. Large or small floral prints, geometric designs and even novelty prints can be showcased in this layout. The bold graphic fabric used as the big-print fabric in the sample was available in a white or black background. Both were incorporated into the quilt with a calmer blue and white to tone things down. To keep things from getting boring, a splash of orange livens it all up! *Consider making this quilt using the following types of fabric: packed prints, directional prints or novelty prints. You could also showcase embroidered blocks, appliqué blocks or photo transfers.*

Cutting Instructions

Note: All strips are cut across the width of the fabric.

FROM THE BIG-PRINT FABRIC, CUT:

27 6½" strips. Set aside **12** strips for the border. Sub cut the **15** remaining strips into **90** 6½" squares.

FROM THE ACCENT FABRIC #1, CUT:

14 6½" strips. Sub cut into **84** 6½" squares.

FROM THE ACCENT FABRIC #2, CUT:

10 6½" strips. Sub cut into **60** 6½" squares.

FROM THE ACCENT #3, CUT:

5 6½" strips. Cross cut into **30** 6½" squares.
10 2½" strips for inner border.
12 2¼" strips for binding.

While it's great to have multiple sizes of rulers at your fingertips, sometimes you don't have one that's wide enough for the strips you need to cut. If you only have a 6" wide ruler, but need to cut 6½" strips, try laying two rulers side by side to give you the width you require.

Piecing the Top

1 Work on a design wall or on the floor. Refer to the Assembly Diagram. Lay out the blocks to create a Trip-Around-The-World pattern.

Note: There will be nine blocks left over.

2 Once the blocks have been arranged, join them together in rows.

3 Press the seams in each row in opposite directions. This will allow the seams in each row to next wit the seams in the row below it.

4 Join the rows together, starting from the top of the quilt down. Press.

Assembly Diagram

You will have nine squares left over when you are finished piecing your quilt top. These could easily be sewn into a nine-patch block and used to make a coordinating throw pillow.

Adding the Borders

1 Join the strips for the inner border together by sewing diagonal seams. Press open. Join all of the strips together until you have one long strip.

2 Measure the length of the quilt lengthwise *through the middle.* This will prevent you from having wavy borders. Mathematically this number would be 102½", but everyone's seam allowances vary, so be sure to measure.

3 Cut two strips the length of the quilt. Attach one to each side of the quilt. Press.

4 Now measure the quilt crosswise *through the middle.* This measurement should be approximately 94½", but check your measurement to be sure.

5 Cut two strips this length. Attach one to the top and one to the bottom of the quilt. Press. Repeat Steps 1–4 with the outer border fabric. Be sure to measure, and use your calculation in Step 2.

Finishing Your Quilt

1 Cut your backing fabric into three equal pieces. Remove selvages and join together.

2 Prepare your quilt sandwich following the Layering and Basting instructions on page 12.

3 Sometimes, as in the sample, the pattern in the fabric can dictate the quilting design. The great Art Deco lines of the fabrics prompted me to quilt an all over geometric design.

This quilt would also be a good candidate for stitching in the ditch. Other options include diagonal quilting through each row of squares or an all over design.

4 Bind and label your quilt following the instructions on page 13.

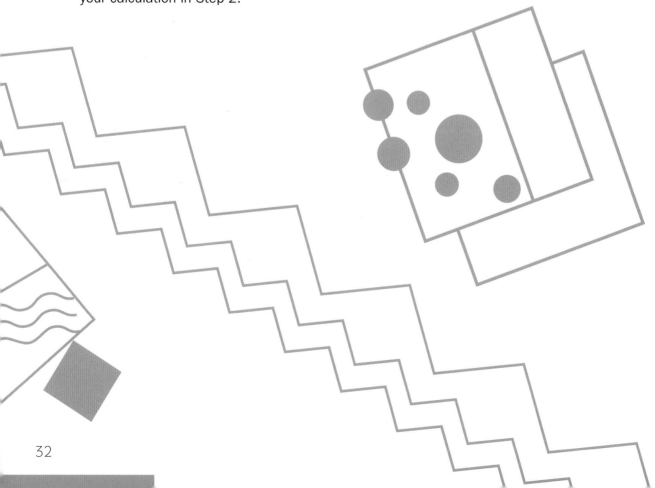

Grand Daddy

A crisp look is achieved in this quilt because of the strong contrast between the packed floral and the background fabrics.

Pieced by Connie Nason and quilted by the author.

It's so interesting to think about the names that were given to quilt blocks by our grandmothers, and their grandmothers before them. So often they reflected the everyday objects found around the home or farm—maple leaf, windmill, grandmother's fan—or this one, saw tooth. The famous photographer, Edward S. Curtis, who documented the logging industry in the Northwest, said, "You aren't a logger until you have a one dollar pocket watch and your picture taken with a tree." Luckily, I have a few pictures of my grandfather taken in the woods, back in the days when it took two men and a very big saw to bring down the big trees. It was saws like those that undoubtedly inspired the name of this block.

Measurements

Quilt: 77" x 91"
Block: 10"

Fabric Requirements

- 5¼ yd. big-print fabric for blocks and border
- 2¼ yd. gold accent fabric
- 2½ yd. black for side setting triangles, inner border and binding
- 5⅓ yd. backing
- 81" x 95" batting

Choosing Fabric

To assure that the saw tooth element of this quilt is crisp there are two design elements to keep in mind. The accent fabric that is used for the half-square triangles should contrast sharply with the big-print fabric and the colors in the big-print fabric should be similar in value or intensity. While scale isn't an issue, a packed design for the big-print fabric is preferable. The accent fabric should be a solid, or a fabric that reads as a solid.

With its six inch center, the saw tooth can be used to showcase a special fabric. Here a tightly packed floral seemed just the thing to use to showcase all the sharp teeth created by the half-square triangles. If you chose to use this pattern for embroidered or appliqué blocks, match the saw tooth points to the background of the featured blocks. *Consider making this quilt using the following type of fabric: packed*

prints. You could also showcase embroidered blocks, appliqué blocks or photo transfers.

Cutting Instructions

Note: *All strips are cut across the width of the fabric.*
Note: *For ease of construction, use the Gridded Triangle Method on page 15.*

FROM THE BIG-PRINT FABRIC, CUT:

4   15" strips for gridded triangles. Sub cut into **13** rectangles, 15" x 9".*
6   6½" strips. Sub cut into **32** 6½" squares.
4   2½" strips. Sub cut into **64** 2½" squares.
8   8½" strips for outer border.

FROM THE ACCENT FABRIC, CUT:

4   15" strips for gridded triangles. Sub cut into **13** rectangles, 15" x 9".*
4   2½" strips. Sub cut into **64** 2½" squares.

FROM THE INNER BORDER, CUT:

7   2½" strips.
3   14¼" strips. Sub cut into **5** 14¼" squares. Cut each square in half twice diagonally to make **20** side-setting triangles. From the remainder of the strips cut **2** 8" squares. Cut each square once diagonally for corner triangles.
9   2¼" strips for binding.

*If not using the Gridded Triangle Method, cut **15**, 2⅞" strips. Sub cut into **192** 2⅞" squares.*

Piecing the Blocks

1 See page 15 for instructions on Gridded Triangle Method. Make 384 half-square triangles. Press and trim dog ears from triangles.

Fig. 1. Half-square triangle. Make 384.

2 Join three half-square triangles with the big print to the right as shown in Figure 2. Make 64. Triangle-Strip A.

Fig. 2. Triangle-Strip A. Make 64.

3 Join three half-square triangles with the big print to the left as shown in Figure 3. Make 64. Triangle-Strip B.

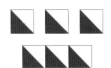

Fig. 3. Triangle-Strip B. Make 64.

4 Add a 2½" accent square and a 2½" big-print square to either side of a Triangle-Strip B as shown in Figure 4. Be sure the accent square is on the left of Triangle-Strip B and the big-print square is on the right. Make 64.

Fig. 4. Add a 2½" accent square and a 2½" big-print square to either side of a Triangle-Strip B. Make 64.

5 Join a Triangle-Strip A to each side of a 6½" big-print square as shown in Figure 5. Be sure the big-print triangle is toward the 6½" big-print square. Press the seam allowances toward center.

Fig. 5. Add a Triangle-Strip A to each side of a 6½" square.

6 Join a Triangle-Strip B (with the additional 2½" squares) to each side of the block from Step 5. Be sure the big-print triangles are toward the 6½" big-print square and that the 2½" big-print squares are in opposite corners. Press the seam allowances toward center. Make 32 blocks.

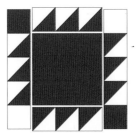

Fig. 6. Add a triangle-strip B to each side of a 6½" square. Make 32 blocks.

Dog ears are the little points of fabric that extend beyond the seams when making half-square triangles. Trimming them makes a neater block and allows for easier matching of seams. A quick and easy way to trim dog ears is to place the pieced half-square triangle on a cutting mat before pressing it open. With the dog ears to the right and top, position a square ruler to the right top edge and cut off ears. The square is trimmed and the waste stays on the mat for easy clean up.

Assembling the Top

1 Working on a design wall or on the floor, lay out the Sawtooth blocks and setting triangles as shown in the Assembly Diagram.

2 Join blocks together in diagonal rows.

3 Press the seams in each row in opposite directions. This will allow the seams in each row to nest with the seams in the row below it.

4 Join the rows together. Press.

Assembly Diagram

Adding the Borders

1. Join the strips for the inner border together by sewing diagonal seams. Press open. Join all of the strips together until you have one long strip.

2. Measure the length of the quilt lengthwise *through the middle.* This will prevent you from having wavy borders. Mathematically this number would be 57½", but everyone's seam allowances vary, so be sure to measure. Cut two strips the length of the quilt. Attach one to each side of the quilt. Press.

3. Now measure the quilt crosswise *through the middle.* This measurement should be approximately 75½", but check your measurement to be sure. Cut two strips this length. Attach one to the top and one to the bottom of your quilt. Press.

4. Repeat Steps 1–3 with your outer border fabric. Be sure to measure.

Finishing Your Quilt

1. Cut the backing fabric into two equal pieces. Remove selvages and join together.

2. Prepare your quilt sandwich following the Layering and Basting instructions on page 12.

3. Depending on how busy the print is in your big-print fabric, the large center squares and wide borders on this quilt could lend themselves to some special quilting. However, if the print you chose is very busy the work you put into the quilting may not be apparent. In such cases I often choose to do an allover design like a stipple or pantograph. Because of the strong contrast between the big-print fabric and the gold background I chose not to do any quilting in the gold and quilted the rest of the quilt with a stipple in black thread.

4. Bind and label your quilt following the instructions on page 13.

Hercules

Cutting this big-print up didn't curtail the action of the Wild West print!

Pieced by Beverly Wakeman and quilted by the author.

This star, with its skinny arms and legs, goes by many names but it has always reminded me of Hercules holding up the world. It may look like the star is the block, but in this quilt, it is actually the sashing. That leaves a big, 9½" square to be the starring block—a perfect place to showcase a big print or novelty fabric.

Measurements

Quilt: 75" x 87"
Block: 9"

Fabric Requirements

- 3⅝ yd. big-print fabric
- 1¼ yd. blender fabric
- ¾ yd. red accent fabric #1
- ⅔ yd. gold accent fabric #2
- ⅞ yd. medium brown inner border
- 5⅛ yd. backing
- ⅝ yd. dark brown binding
- 79" x 91" batting

Note: *For this quilt you will need to trace templates A and B onto template plastic. Or you could invest in a set of acrylic templates made just for cutting these two shapes, like the Tri-Recs ruler.*

Choosing Fabric

The long-legged stars used in Hercules serve as a focal design element and break up the big print. Their skinny nature, however, leaves large connecting squares that are the perfect place to let the big-print fabric shine. This area could be filled with a beautiful, bold floral or something fun like the cowboy print used in the sample. The 9 square could also be used to showcase embroidered or appliquéd blocks.

I wanted the design of the cowboy print to flow like it did when I rolled the fabric off the bolt. To accomplish this I cut some elements cross grain and some elements lengthwise. *Consider making this quilt using the following type of fabrics: packed prints, directional prints or novelty prints. You could also showcase embroidered blocks, appliqué blocks, photo transfers or T-shirt blocks.*

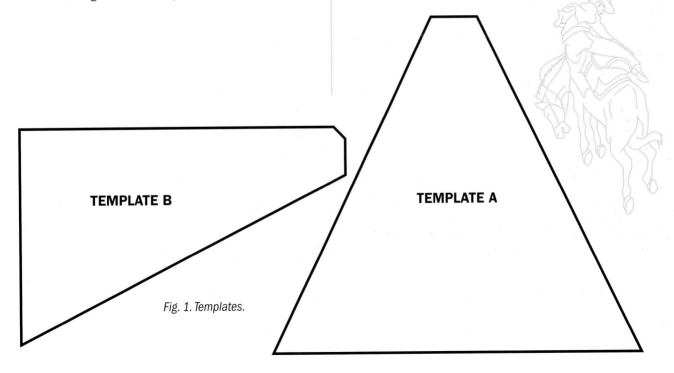

TEMPLATE B

TEMPLATE A

Fig. 1. Templates.

Cutting Instructions

Note: *All strips are cut across the width of the fabric.*

FROM THE BIG-PRINT FABRIC, CUT:

5 9½" strips. Sub cut into **20** 9½" squares.
3 6½" strips for top and bottom border.

NOW TURN THE FABRIC AND CUT LENGTHWISE STRIPS:

2 6½" x 77" strips for side borders.
2 3½" x 40" strips. Sub cut into **10** rectangles, 3½" x 9½".

FROM REMAINING FABRIC, WHICH SHOULD BE APPROXIMATELY 22 WIDE, CUT CROSS GRAIN:

7 3½" strips. Sub cut into **8** rectangles, 3½" x 9½" and **16** 3½" squares.

FROM THE BLENDER FABRIC, CUT:

5 3½" strips. Sub cut into **49** 3½" squares.
7 3½" strips. Sub cut into **120** Template A pieces.
8 6½" strips for border.

FROM THE ACCENT FABRIC #1, CUT:

4 3½" strips. Lay strips in pairs, right sides together. When cutting, you will get mirror image shapes needed to complete the long-legged stars. Sub cut into **120** Template B pieces.
3 3½" strips. Sub cut into **27** 3½" squares. Set aside **12** for borders.

FROM THE FABRIC #2, CUT:

4 3½" strips. Lay strips in pairs, right sides together. When cutting, you will get mirror image shapes needed to complete the long-legged stars. Sub cut into **120** Template B pieces.
2 3½" strips. Sub cut into **15** 3½" squares.

FROM THE INNER BORDER FABRIC, CUT:

7 3½" strips.

FROM THE BINDING FABRIC, CUT

8 2¼" strips.

Piecing the Units

1 Sew a red Template B piece to each side of a Template A piece as shown in Figure 1. Make 60.

2 Sew a gold Template B piece to each side of a Template A piece. Make 60.

**UNIT A-RED.
MAKE 60.**   **UNIT A-GOLD.
MAKE 60.**

Fig. 2.

2 Join a Unit A-Red and a Unit A-Gold to either side of a 3½" square of blender fabric as shown in Figure 3. This is Unit B. Make 49.

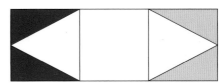

UNIT B. MAKE 49.

Fig. 3.

Assembling the Top

1 Working on a design wall or on the floor, lay out the pieced Tri-Recs units, sashing pieces and big print fabric blocks as shown in the Assembly Diagram.

2 Join the blocks together in rows. (Figure 4 shows you how many rows of each row set you will need.)

3 Press the sashing rows toward the star centers and the block rows toward the 9½" squares. This will allow the seams in each row to nest with the seams in the row below it.

4 Join the rows together. Press.

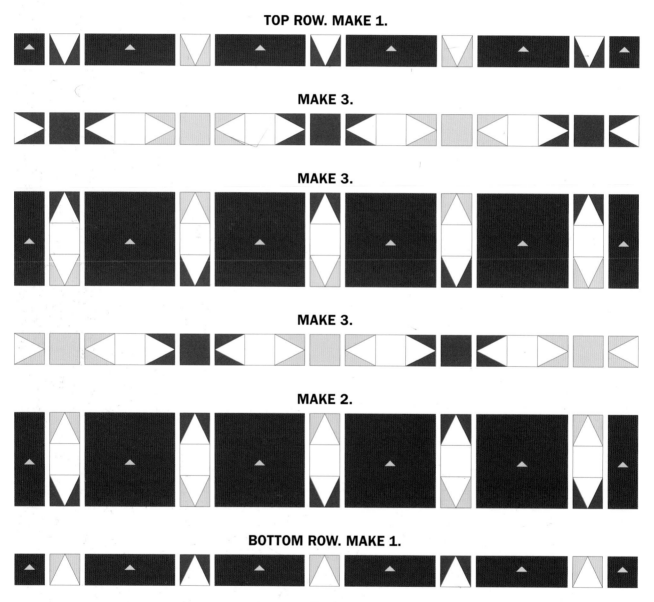

Fig. 4.

Assembly Diagram

Adding the Borders

INNER BORDER

1 Join the strips for the inner border together by sewing diagonal seams. Press open. Join all of the strips together until you have one long strip.

2 Measure the length of the quilt lengthwise *through the middle*. This will prevent you from having wavy borders. Mathematically this number would be 69½" but everyone's seam allowances vary, so be sure to measure. Cut two strips this length.

3 Before adding borders to the side of the quilt, measure the top crosswise *through the middle*. This measurement should be 57½" but check your measurement to be sure.

4 Cut two strips this length. Add a 3½" square of accent fabric #1 to each end of these strips.

5 Attach borders from Step 2 to each side of the quilt. Press. Attach borders from Step 4 to the top and bottom of the quilt. Press.

OUTER BORDER

1 Join two 3½" squares of outer border fabric with two 3½" squares of accent fabric #1 to make a four-patch. Make 4.

2 Join the strips for the outer border together. Press seams open. Join all of the strips together until you have one long strip.

3 Measure the length of the quilt top lengthwise *through the middle*. This will prevent you from having wavy borders. Mathematically this number would be 75½" but everyone's seam allowances vary, so be sure to measure. Cut two strips this length.

4 Before adding borders to side of quilt, measure the top crosswise *through the middle*. This measurement should be 63½" but check your measurement to be sure. Cut two strips this length.

5 Add a four-patch to each end of these strips. Check the orientation of the four-patch, keeping the accent fabric at the outer corners.

6 Attach borders from Step 3 to each side of the quilt. Press. Attach borders from Step 5 to the top and bottom of the quilt. Press.

Finishing Your Quilt

1 Cut the backing fabric into two equal pieces. Remove selvages and join together.

2 Prepare the quilt sandwich following the Layering and Basting instructions on page 12.

3 In a quilt that features a panoramic scene like the one pictured, care needs to be taken to avoid distracting the eye with an obvious quilting pattern. The quilting should enhance both the piecing and the featured fabric. Quilting in the ditch is a perfect way to accomplish this, but the large nine-inch squares will need some additional quilting. In the sample quilt, I took a cue from the fabric and quilted loops and lariats across the surface.

4 Bind and label your quilt following the instructions on page 13.

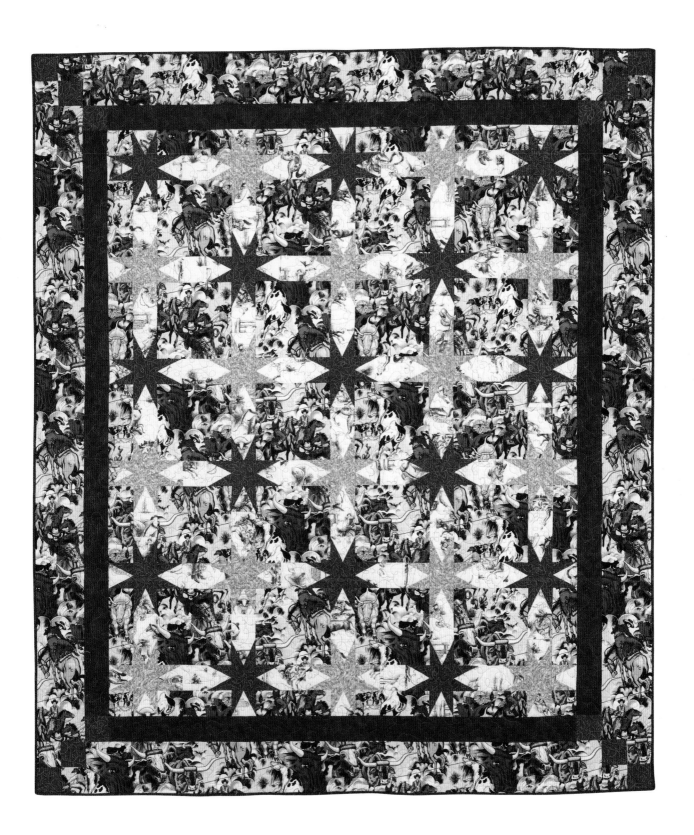

Big Sky

These flying geese have a bird's eye view of the poppy fields below.

Pieced by Connie Nason and quilted by the author.

There's nothing prettier than a wide-open sky filled with migrating geese. Their majestic forms and precision flight patterns are a sight to behold. Quilter's through the generations have been inspired by these formations and created many quilts using the flying geese block. Because there's nothing to interrupt the strong geometric design in the quilt, and with a nod to my Montana-born husband, I've dubbed this quilt Big Sky!

Measurements

Quilt: 76" x 97"
Block: 10"

Fabric Requirements

- 4⅞ yd. big-print fabric
- 1½ yd. green accent fabric
- 2⅓ yd. black for border and binding
- 5⅔ yd. backing fabric
- 80" x 101" batting

Choosing Fabric

This design allows the quilter to take advantage of an open design like the poppy print but would work just as well with a packed floral or other print.

Although the poppy print is very large scale I used it for the background of the flying geese so they would appear to float across the quilt's top. A solid black fabric would have been a good alternative and would have created a "harder" line in the design.

The large, 10" squares in this design leave room for other options. *Consider making this quilt using the following type of fabrics: packed prints, scattered prints or novelty prints. You could also showcase embroidered blocks, appliqué blocks, photo transfers or T-shirt blocks.*

Cutting Instructions

Note: All strips are cut across the width of the fabric.

FROM THE BIG-PRINT FABRIC, CUT:

5 10½" strips. Sub cut into **17** 10½" squares.

2 14¼" strips. Sub cut into **4** 14¼" squares. Cut each square twice diagonally for **16** large side setting triangles.

1 7⅛" strip. Sub cut into **3** 7⅛" squares. Cut each square twice diagonally for **12** small side setting triangles. From the remaining strip cut **2** 4½" squares. Cut each square in half diagonally for four corner setting triangles.

16 3⅜" strips. Sub cut into **192** 3⅜" squares, for flying geese.

3 5½" strips. Sub cut into **18** 5½" squares.

1 3⅞" strip. Sub cut into **4** 3⅞" squares.

1 3½" strip. Sub cut into **8** 3½" squares.

FROM THE ACCENT FABRIC, CUT:

8 6¼" strips. Sub cut into **48** 6¼" squares, for flying geese.

FROM THE BORDER FABRIC, CUT:

8 6½" strips.

1 3⅞" strip. Sub cut into **4** 3⅞" squares.

9 2¼" x 40" for binding.

Piecing the Blocks

Note: The "blocks" in this quilt are really pieced sashing units that frame the 10 squares.

FLYING GEESE

Note: I've made flying geese by many different methods, and my poor geese always looked like they had one broken wing. Then I discovered this method, and now I always make my geese this way. Besides making perfect geese, you get four geese at a time! If you like this method, there's a great ruler called the Flying Geese x 4 Ruler that takes the math out of making the blocks.

1   Place two 3⅜" squares of big-print fabric on opposite corners of a 6¼" accent square. Draw a diagonal line through the small squares as shown in Figure 1.

Note: *the squares will overlap slightly in the center.*

Fig. 1.

2   Sew a scant ¼" on either side of the marked line. Cut apart on the marked line as shown in Figure 2. You will have two pieces as shown in Figure 3. Press toward the big-print fabric.

Fig. 2.

Fig. 3.

3   Place a 3⅜" square on one of the two units. Draw a diagonal line through the small square, and sew a scant ¼" on either side of the marked line. Cut apart on the marked line as shown in Figure 4. Press toward the big-print fabric. Repeat with second unit.

Fig. 4.

4   Repeat to make 48 sets. You will end up with 192 flying geese as shown in Figure 5.

Fig. 5. Make 192.

5   Join four flying geese together to make a sashing unit as shown in Figure 6. Make 48 sashing units.

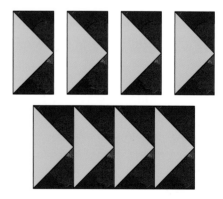

Fig. 6. Make 48 sashing units.

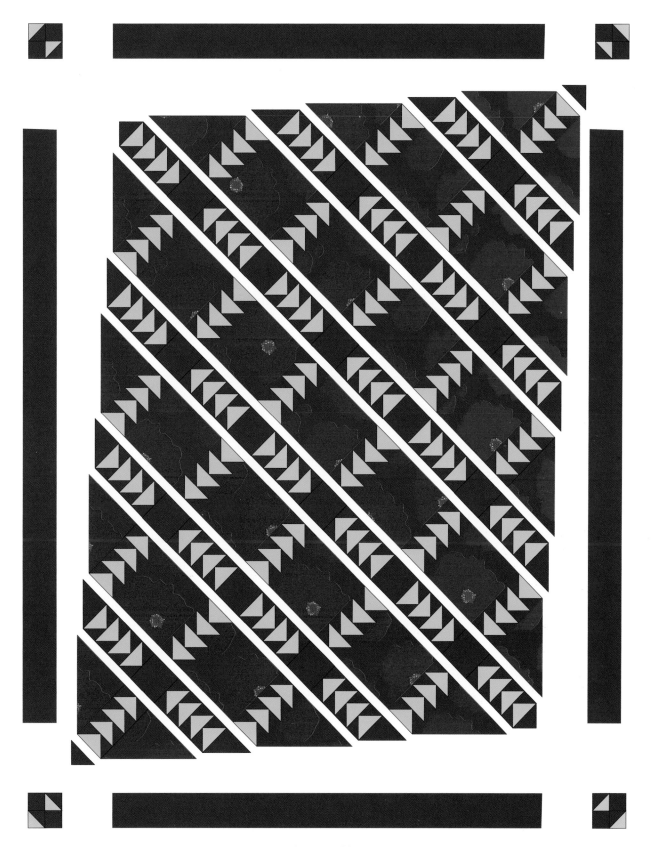

Assembly Diagram

Assembling the Top

1 Working on a design wall or on the floor, lay out the 10½" blocks and sashing (Flying Geese) units in diagonal rows. See Assembly Diagram on page 51.

2 Add setting and corner triangles.

3 Join the blocks together in rows. Press toward the big print fabric. This will allow the seams in each row to next with the seams in the next row.

4 Join the diagonal rows together. Press.

Piecing the Corners

1 Draw a diagonal line on the wrong side of a 3⅞" square of accent fabric. Place the square on a 3⅞" square of border fabric with right sides together.

2 Sew a scant ¼" on either side of the drawn line, and cut on the marked line. Press toward the border fabric. Yields 2 half-square triangles. Repeat with the remaining 3⅞" squares to make 8 half-square triangles as shown in Figure 7.

Fig. 7. Half-square triangle. Make 8.

3 Add a 3½" square of border fabric to opposite sides of two half-square triangles. Press toward the border fabric. Join together to make a four-patch. Make 4.

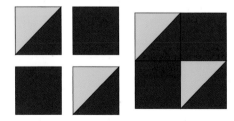

Fig. 8. Pieced corner construction.

Borders

1 Join the strips for the border together by sewing diagonal seams. Press open. Join all of the strips together until you have one long strip.

2 Measure the length of the quilt lengthwise *through the middle.* This will prevent you from having wavy borders. Mathematically this number would be approximately 85", but everyone's seam allowances vary, so be sure to measure. Cut two strips the length of your quilt.

3 Before adding borders to the side of the quilt, measure the top crosswise *through the middle.* This measurement should be 64" but check your measurement to be sure. Cut two strips this length.

4 Add a four-patch to each end of these strips. Check the orientation of the four-patch, keeping the accent fabric at the inner corners.

5 Attach borders from Step 2 to each side of the quilt. Press. Attach borders from Step 4 to the top and bottom of the quilt. Press.

Finishing Your Quilt

1 Cut the backing fabric into two equal pieces. Remove selvages and join together.

2 Prepare the quilt sandwich following the Layering and Basting instructions on page 12.

3 If you have strong contrast between your big-print fabric and your accent fabric, you might consider using two different colors of threads to quilt this quilt, matching each thread to the fabrics. Or quilt only in the areas of the big-print fabric and leave the accent fabric, the geese, unquilted entirely.

4 Bind and label your quilt following the instructions on page 13.

Big Thunder

Black and red are a stunning combination in this streak-of-lightning design.

Pieced by Carol Osterholm and quilted by the author.

Streak of Lightening is one of the most stunning quilt settings. Whether you're setting together pieced blocks or showcasing a fantastic print, this setting is dramatic. While it may look tricky, all you do is create strips with side setting triangles. Once the strips are completed, simply join them together!

Measurements

Quilt: 75" x 89"
Block: 10"

Fabric Requirements

- 4¼ yd. big-print fabric
- 2½ yd. black accent fabric
- ⅜ yd. red inner border
- 5¼ yd. backing
- 79" x 93" batting

Choosing Fabric

Black and red always make a dramatic color combination. Pairing those two colors with a graphic setting like Streak of Lightening makes a very bold statement. Other exciting combinations would be yellow and blue, pink and brown or lime and black. If you prefer something calmer, consider a romantic floral for your big-print fabric and a soft pastel for the streak of lightening.

This quilt is a great way to feature a bold fabric like the print shown. The simplicity of the setting, though, also means it would be the perfect place to feature some special blocks. *Consider making this quilt using the following type of fabrics: scattered prints, packed prints or novelty prints. You could also showcase sampler blocks, embroidered blocks, appliqué blocks, photo transfers or T-shirt blocks.*

Cutting Instructions

Note: All strips are cut across the width of the fabric.

FROM THE BIG-PRINT FABRIC, CUT:

- **6** 10½" strips. Sub cut into **22** 10½" squares.
- **1** 4½" strip. Sub cut into **4** 4½" squares.
- **7** 8¼" strips for border.
- **9** 2¼" strips for binding.

FROM THE BLACK FABRIC, CUT:

- **5** 14¼" strips. Sub cut into **10** 14¼" squares. Cut each square in half twice diagonally to make **36** side setting triangles. From the remainder of the strips cut **4** 8" squares. Cut each square once diagonally for corner triangles.
- **2** 6" strips. Sub cut into **8** 6" squares. Cut each square once diagonally.

FROM THE RED FABRIC, CUT:

- **7** 1½" strips.

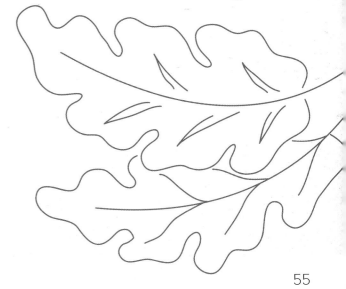

Piecing the Strips

ROWS 1 AND 3

1 Lay out 5 squares of big print fabric, side setting triangles and corner triangles.

Fig. 1. Layout, Rows 1 and 3.

2 Join in diagonal rows. Press toward the setting triangles.

Fig. 2. Diagonal Assembly, Rows 1 and 3.

3 Join rows together. Press.

ROWS 2 AND 4

1 Lay out 6 squares of big print fabric, 10 side setting triangles and corner triangles.

Fig. 3. Layout, Rows 2 and 4.

2 Join in diagonal rows. Press toward the setting triangles.

Fig. 4. Diagonal Assembly, Rows 2 and 4.

3 Join rows together. Press.

4 Draw a diagonal line through the top and bottom square in each row.

Note: *This is NOT the cutting line.*

5 Sew ⅛" outside the marked line to stabilize the bias edge.

6 Trim edges, being sure to leave a ¼" seam allowance.

Assembling the Top

1 Join rows 1 and 2. Press. See Assembly Diagram on page 58.

2 Join rows 3 and 4. Press.

3 Join the two sections together. Press.

Adding the Borders

INNER BORDER

1 Join the strips for the inner border together by sewing diagonal seams. Press open. Join all of the strips together until you have one long strip.

2 Measure the length of the quilt lengthwise *through the middle.* This will prevent you from having wavy borders. Mathematically this number would be 71½" but everyone's seam allowances vary, so be sure to measure.

3 Cut two strips the length of the quilt. Attach one to each side of the quilt. Press.

4 Now measure the quilt crosswise *through the middle.* This measurement should be approximately 59½" but check your measurement to be sure. Cut two strips this length. Add them to the top and bottom of your quilt. Press.

PIECED CORNERS

1 To each side of a 4½" square of big-print fabric, add a 6" black triangle as shown in Figure 5. Press toward the triangle.

2 Add a 6" black triangle to each remaining side. Press. Square to 8½" if necessary. Make 4.

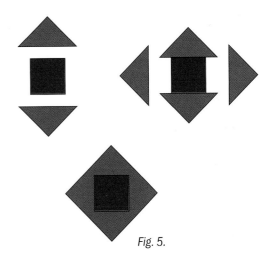

Fig. 5.

OUTER BORDER

1 Join the strips for the outer border together by sewing diagonal seams. Press open. Join all of the strips together until you have one long strip.

2 Measure the length of the quilt top lengthwise *through the middle.* This will prevent you from having wavy borders. Mathematically this number would be 73½" but everyone's seam allowances vary, so be sure to measure.

3 Before adding borders to the side of the quilt, measure the top crosswise *through the middle.* This measurement should be 59½" but check your measurement to be sure.

4 Cut two strips this length. Add a corner unit to each end of these strips.

5 Attach borders from Step 2 to each side of the quilt. Press. Attach borders from Step 4 to the top and one to the bottom of your quilt. Press.

Finishing Your Quilt

1   Cut the backing fabric into two equal pieces. Remove selvages and join together.

2   Prepare your quilt sandwich following the Layering and Basting instructions on page 12.

3   This quilt is finished with a small stipple design stitched with black thread. The long, linear elements of this quilt could be reinforced with straight-line quilting that follows the angles of the design. If there is strong contrast in the two fabrics used, a change of quilting thread may be in order.

4   Bind and label your quilt following the instructions on page 13.

When using dark fabrics, especially solid black, choose a black batting for your quilt. When quilting, the needle and thread can pull small bits of the batting fiber through to the top of the quilt. White or cream colored battings could detract from the beauty of your quilt.

Assembly Diagram

Grandeur

Even though the piecing is simple, the variety of sizes and shapes of the blocks in this quilt keep it interesting.

Pieced and quilted by the author.

This quilt really shows off the beautiful floral fabric. The irregular placement of the sashings create interest but don't detract from the design in the large-scale print. The subtle colors of the sashing and inner border also keep the design calm. This quilt also has a pieced back that incorporates strips left over from cutting the fabrics for the quilt top.

Measurements

Quilt: 68" x 80"

Fabric Requirements

- 4½ yd. big-print fabric
- 1⅝ yd. green sashing fabric
- ½ yd. red inner border fabric
- ¾ yd. binding
- 72" x 84" batting
- 5 yd. backing

Choosing Fabric

The large floral fabric used in this quilt was directional but a carefully thought out cutting plan keeps the elements flowing. While this is a splendid way to use a big, beautiful floral print, the sashing also reminds me of strips of film. Why not try incorporating photo transfers in this project? *Consider making this quilt using the following type of fabrics: scattered prints, directional prints or novelty prints. You could also showcase embroidered blocks, appliqué blocks, photo transfers or T-shirt blocks.*

Cutting Instructions

FROM THE BIG-PRINT FABRIC, CUT:

Note: You may want to keep track of the layout of the big-print fabric and re-assemble it in the same order that it was before cutting.

1   Cut a 54" piece. Open it, press and trim away the selvages.

2   Turn the fabric lengthwise and cut five strips in this order: 8½", 6½", 8½", 6½", 8½".

3   From the 8½" strips cut **4, 8½" x 13"** rectangles.

4   From the 6½" strips cut, *in order,* **1** 6½" square, **2** 6½" x 12½" rectangles, and **1** 6½" square.

5   From the remaining big-print fabric, cut, selvage to selvage, **4** strips 8½" for top and bottom border and corners. Set aside three strips for the border.

6   From the fourth strip, cut **4** 6½" squares, fussy cutting if desired.

7   Turn the remaining fabric and cut **2, 8½"** x 60½" strips for side borders.

Note: The remaining big-print fabric could be used on the back of the quilt.

FROM THE GREEN FABRIC, CUT:

22   2½" strips. Set aside **12** strips for piecing.

From the remaining **10** strips cut 9 2½" x 8½" rectangles, **16** 2½" x 6½" rectangles, and **8** 2½" x 10½" rectangles.

FROM THE RED FABRIC, CUT:

6   2½" strips.

FROM THE BINDING, CUT:

8   2¼" strips.

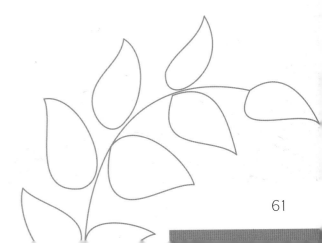

Grandeur

Piecing the Top

CENTER

1 Working on a design wall or the floor, lay out the center of the quilt.

2 Alternate rows of larger blocks and smaller blocks. See Assembly Diagram.

3 Add 8½" and 6½" (based on the width of each particular row) horizontal sashings between the blocks. Join together in rows. Press toward the blocks.

4 Join together twelve 2½" sashing strips by sewing diagonal seams. Press seams open.

5 From this long strip cut six 2½" x 56½" strips for vertical sashing and two 2½" x 48½" for horizontal sashing. See Assembly Diagram.

6 Add the vertical sashing strips between the rows of the blocks and to the outside edges. Press.

7 Add the horizontal sashing strips to the top and bottom. Press.

CORNERS

1 Sew a 2½" x 6½" green strip to opposite sides of a 6½" x 6½" corner square. Press.

2 Sew a 2½" x 10½" green strip to the top and bottom of the square. Press.

3 Repeat to make four corners.

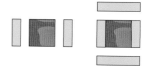

Border corner unit. Make 4.

Assembly Diagram

Adding the Borders

1 Join the red strips for the pieced border together by sewing diagonal seams. Press open. Join all of the strips together until you have one long strip. From this long strip cut two 2½" x 52½" strips and two 2½" x 60½" strips.

2 Join the three strips of horizontal border fabric together, matching pattern as possible. Cut into two 8½" x 52½" strips.

3 Trim vertical borders to 60½".

4 Join a red strip to one side of each of the border strips.

5 Sew the vertical border strips to the quilt top with the red strip to the inside.

6 Add a corner square to each end of the horizontal borders. Sew the horizontal border strips to the quilt top with the red strip to the inside.

Finishing Your Quilt

1 Cut your backing fabric into two equal pieces.* Remove selvages and join together. Prepare your quilt sandwich following the Layering and Basting instructions on page 12.

2 An all over design would work nicely on this quilt as long as the color of the thread doesn't detract from the fabrics. Bind and label your quilt following the instructions on page 13.

* Incorporate remaining big print fabric if desired.

Picture Window

These robots had been in my stash for several years before I found a perfect way to feature them.

Pieced and quilted by the author.

In this quilt, blocks are framed on two sides to give the illusion of looking through a window. Pesky "Y" seams are avoided by using half-square triangles in the corners. This is one of the quickest quilts to stitch up and is an excellent way to feature novelty prints.

Measurements

Quilt: 62" x 90"
Block: 12"

Fabric Requirements

- 1¼ yd. big-print fabric—more if fussy cutting
- 2¼ yd. red for left frame and outer border
- 1⅓ yd. gray bottom frame and middle border
- 1⅔ yd. black for sashing and binding
- 5¼ yd. backing
- 66" x 94" batting

Choosing Fabric

When wanting to showcase a novelty print there's probably no better pattern to use than the Attic Window. If you choose a packed design, strip cutting will work perfectly. However, if you have a larger, tossed design plan to buy extra fabric and fussy cut the large squares.

The framing fabrics should do just what the name implies—frame the blocks. To give the proper perspective to the design be sure to use two very different colors or values in your two framing fabrics. Because you want the half-square triangles to give the illusion of "Y" seams in the corners, a solid, marbled or small-scale print should be chosen. *Consider making this quilt using the following type of fabrics: scattered prints, directional prints or novelty prints. You could also showcase embroidered blocks, appliqué blocks, sampler blocks, photo transfers or T-shirt blocks.*

Cutting Instructions

Note: All strips are cut across the width of the fabric.

FROM THE BIG-PRINT FABRIC, CUT:

4   9½" strips. Sub cut into **15** 9½ " squares.

Note: If using a novelty print you may want to fussy cut the squares.

FROM THE RED FABRIC, CUT:

1   3⅞" strip. Sub cut into **8** 3⅞" squares.
4   3½" strips. Sub cut into **15** 3½" x 9½" rectangles.
8   6½" strips for outer border.

FROM THE GRAY FABRIC, CUT:

1   3⅞" strip. Sub cut into **8** 3⅞" squares.
4   3½" strips. Sub cut into **15** 3½" x 9½" rectangles.
7   3½" strips for middle border.

FROM THE BLACK FABRIC, CUT:

14   2½" strips. Sub cut into **10** 2½" x 2½" rectangles. (**4** strips will be used for borders.)
8   2¼" strips for sashing.

65

Piecing the Blocks

1 Draw a diagonal line on the wrong side of a 3⅞" red square. Place on a 3⅞" gray square with right sides together. Stitch ¼" on either side of diagonal line. Cut on drawn line. Press. Repeat to make 15 half-square triangles as shown in Figure 1.

Fig. 1. Half-square triangles. Make 15.

2 Join a half-square triangle to the left end of a 3½" x 9½" gray rectangle, checking for orientation of the half-square triangle as shown in Figure 2.

Fig. 2. Check for orientation of the half-square triangle before sewing.

3 Join a 3½" x 9½" red rectangle to the left side of a 9½" square of big-print fabric. Then join a rectangle from Step 2 to the bottom of the pieces as shown in Figure 3. Make 15.

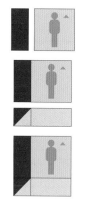

Fig. 3. Make 15 blocks.

Assembling the Top

1 Join three blocks to two 2½" x 12½" sashing strips as shown in Figure 4 to make a row. Press toward the sashing. Make 5 rows.

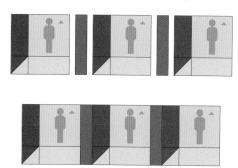

Fig. 4. Make 5 rows.

2 Join rows together with 2½" x 40½" strips of sashing as shown in Figure 5.

3 Sew remaining sashing strips into pairs. Cut to 72½". Add a 72½" strip to each side of the quilt top as shown in Assembly Diagram.

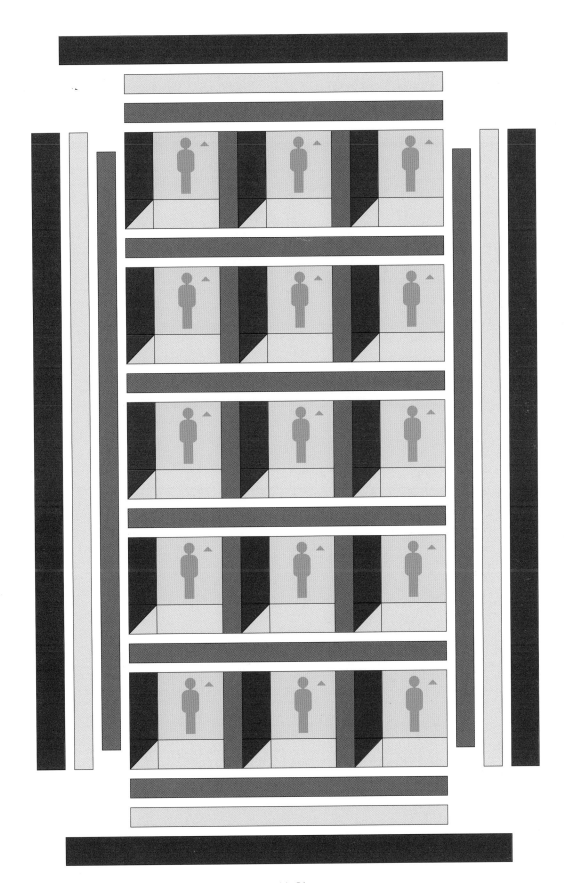

Assembly Diagram

Adding the Borders

1 Join the strips for the inner border together by sewing diagonal seams. Press open. Join all of the strips together until you have one long strip. Measure the length of the quilt lengthwise *through the middle.* This will prevent you from having wavy borders. Mathematically this number would be 72½", but everyone's seam allowances vary, so be sure to measure.

2 Cut two strips the length of your quilt. Attach one to each side of the quilt. Press. Now measure the quilt crosswise *through the middle.* This measurement should be approximately 50½", but check your measurement to be sure.

3 Cut two strips this length. Add them to the top and bottom of your quilt. Press. Repeat Steps 1–4 with your outer border fabric.

Finishing Your Quilt

1 Cut the backing fabric into two equal pieces. Remove selvages and join together.

2 Prepare your quilt sandwich following the Layering and Basting instructions on page 12.

3 If you've gone to the trouble of fussy cutting the big-print fabric or using photo transfers, you'll want to be sure not to detract from the designs with the quilting. Careful selection of thread color and place-ment of stitches will help. Plan to quilt around the designs rather than through them, then do a bit more quilting in the frames, sashing and borders.

4 Bind and label your quilt following the instructions on page 13.

See page 8 for an example of this design featuring an embroidered block.

Whopper

The tiny frames help set off the big-print fabric in this quilt.

Pieced by Connie Nason and quilted by the author.

This design was born of a dilemma. I had just one yard of a pretty floral fabric and I didn't want to cut it into small pieces or large, boring squares. The solution was to cut it into different sized squares and rectangles and set them in an asymmetrical design to keep the pattern from being predictable. Multiple-colored, two-inch squares act as a frame for the blocks and since there was no more big-print fabric for the border, they did double duty there, too. The use of two-inch squares means this pattern is easily adapted to a variety of different size blocks. As long as the dimensions of each of the two sides is divisible by two, you can make a successful quilt.

Measurements

Quilt: 54" x 66"

Fabric Requirements

- 1 yd. big-print fabric
- ¼ yd. each of 12 different coordinating prints for the squares
- ¾ yd. accent fabric for framing strips and inner border
- ⅝ yd. binding
- 3¼ yd. backing
- 58" x 70" batting

Choosing Fabric

As the sample shows, this pattern is a perfect way to use a large floral print. The challenge may come in finding twelve coordinating fabrics for the two inch squares. Let the big-print print be your guide and select fabrics that are a shade or two lighter and darker. Your quilt will be more interesting if you chose a variety of scale as well as colors for the small squares. There's even a small plaid in the pictured quilt.

Not only does this pattern work well for floral fabrics, it is a perfect place to feature fussy cut novelty prints or photo transfers. Keep in mind that you can vary the sizes of the large blocks as long as the measurement of each side, when framed, is divisible by two. **Consider making this quilt using the following type of fabrics: scattered prints, directional prints or novelty prints. You** *could also showcase embroidered blocks, appliqué blocks, photo transfers or T-shirt blocks.*

Cutting Instructions

Note: All strips are cut across the width of the fabric.

FROM THE BIG-PRINT FABRIC, CUT:

2   9½" strips. Sub cut into **5** 9½" x 11½" rectangles.

2   5½" strips. Sub cut into **4** 5½" x 7½" rectangles and **6** 5½" squares.

FROM EACH COORDINATING PRINT, CUT:

3   2½" strips. Sub cut into **48** 2½" squares.

FROM THE ACCENT FABRIC, CUT:

13   1" strips.

5   2½" strips for inner border.

FROM THE BINDING, CUT:

7   2¼" strips.

Making the Units

1. Add 1 strips of accent fabric to each side of a 9½" x 11½" big-print block as shown in Figure 1. Press toward the framing strips. Add 1 strips of accent fabric to the top and bottom of the block. Press toward the framing strips. This block will finish at 10" x 12". Make 5.

2. Repeat Step 1 with 5½" x 7½" rectangles and 5½" x 5½" squares. Make 4 rectangles that finish at 6" x 8" and 6 squares that finish at 6" x 6".

Fig. 1.

3. Set aside four 6½" blocks for the boarders.

Assembling the Top

1. Working on a design wall or on the floor, lay out the framed blocks and 2" squares as shown in the Assembly Diagram. Balance the look of the overall quilt by spreading the 2½" blocks from each coordinating fabric evenly through the design.

2. Assemble the blocks into larger units, as shown. Press.

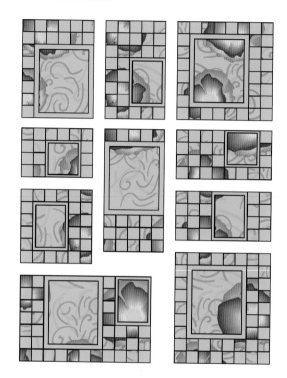

Fig. 2.

3. Join units together to complete the inside of the quilt top. Press.

4. Stay-stitch the edges of the quilt, ¼" from the edge.

Stay stitching stabilizes the edges of your quilt top. A pieced quilt top that doesn't have borders often has many seams along the edges. As you handle your quilt top while basting and quilting it, the stitching at the end of these seams has a tendency to pull apart. To stay stitch, stitch around the outside of your quilt a scant ¼" from the edge. This line of stitching will be covered when you apply your binding.

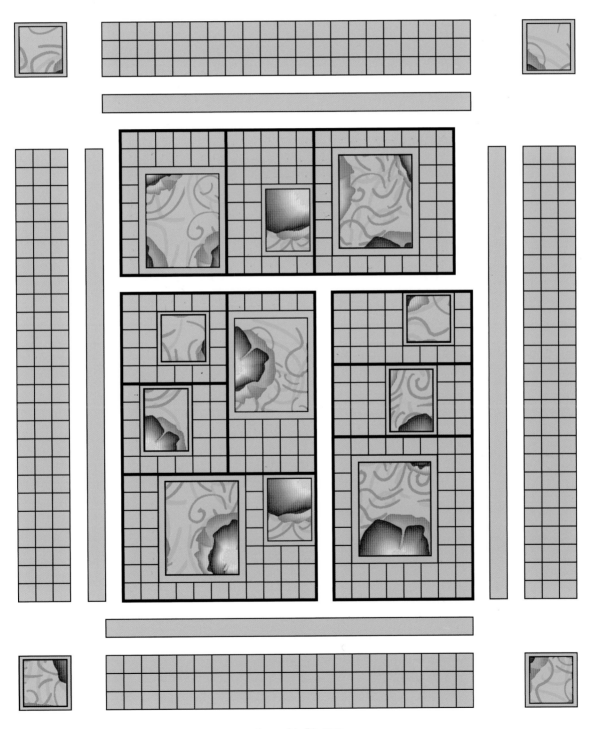

Assembly Diagram

Adding the Inner Borders

1 Cut two border strips to 38½". Add one to the top and one to the bottom of the quilt.

2 Join the remaining three strips together by sewing diagonal seams. Press open.

3 Cut two strips at 54½". Add one strip to each side of the quilt.

Piecing the Outer Borders

1 For a side border, join twenty-seven 2½" squares together into a row. Repeat to make three rows. Press the seams in each row in the opposite direction. This will allow the seams in each row to nest with the seams in the row next to it. Make 2.

2 For the top and bottom borders, join twenty-one 2½" squares together into a row. Repeat to make three rows. Press the seams in each row in the opposite direction. This will allow the seams in each row to nest with the seams in the row below it. Make 2.

3 Add a framed 6½" block to each end of the top and bottom borders.

Adding the Outer Borders

1 Add a pieced border to each side of the quilt. Press toward the inner border.

2 Add the top and bottom pieced borders to the quilt. Press toward the inner border.

Finishing Your Quilt

1 Cut the backing fabric into two equal pieces. Remove selvedges and sew.

2 Prepare your quilt sandwich following the Layering and Basting instructions on page 12.

3 Quilting in the ditch or diagonally through the 2½ squares of this quilt would make a fine finish. In the sample, I took a cue from the acanthus leaves in the big-print fabric. Their graceful curves inspired me to quilt an allover curving design. A combination of hand and machine quilting would also work well here. The majority of this quilt could be machine quilted and some hand quilting could be featured in the larger squares and rectangles.

4 Bind and label your quilt following the instructions on page 13.

See page 9 for an example of this design featuring a photo transfer block.

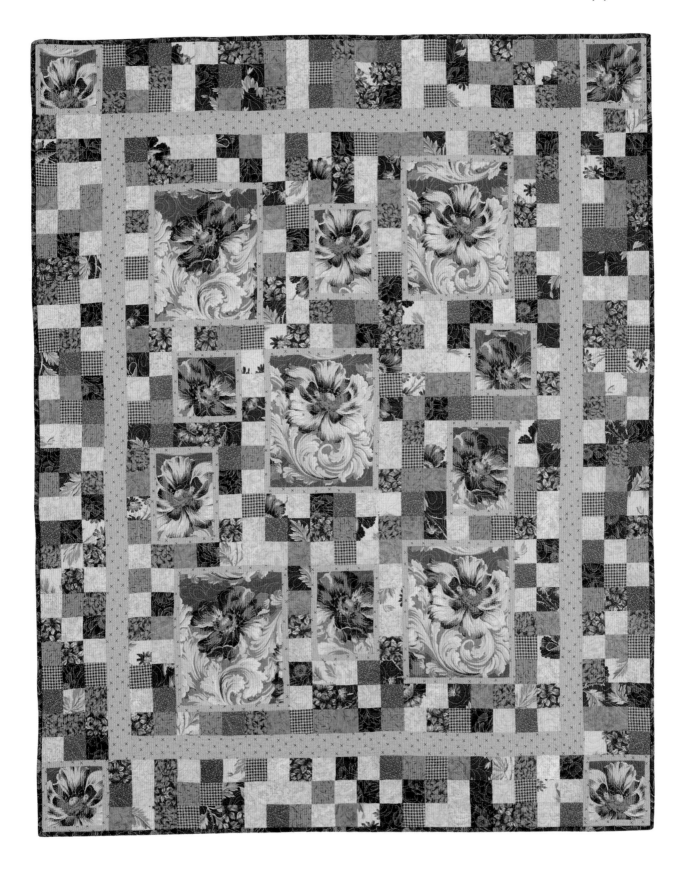

Grand Prix

These fun hot rod prints would please any car buff.

Pieced and quilted by Sue Fair.

Here's a design that will shake things up like the thunder of the engines at an auto race. When framing these rockin' blocks there are no odd angles to cut. The effect is achieved by simply adding strips to the fussy cut blocks. Then, just twist and turn a 12½ square-up ruler over the top, take a couple of easy slices with your rotary cutter and you're ready to take these blocks for a spin!

Measurements

Quilt: 68" x 80"
Block: 12"

Fabric Requirements

- 1⅝ yd. big-print fabric—more if fussy cutting
- 1 yd. accent fabric #1
- 1 yd. accent fabric #2
- ½ yd. inner border
- 1¾ yd. outer border
- 4 yd. backing
- 2/3 yd. binding
- 72" x 84" batting

Choosing Fabric

Here's a chance to use those great novelty prints that could drive a quilter crazy! Whether you're working with dinosaurs, hot rods or pin-up girls, this is the perfect vehicle to showcase the fabric. It would also work well with T-shirts. Since a collection of T-shirts will undoubtedly have different background colors, the frames can act to tie everything together.

If you can find framing fabric that fits the theme of your blocks, like the flame fabric with the hot rods, you'll add to the fun of the quilt. However, if there's nothing to carry out the theme, find a couple of nice blender fabrics. They'll do nicely. **Consider making this quilt using the following type of fabrics: scattered prints, packed prints, directional prints or novelty prints. You could also showcase embroidered blocks, appliqué blocks, photo transfers or T-shirt blocks.**

Cutting Instructions

Note: All strips are cut across the width of the fabric.

FROM THE BIG-PRINT FABRIC, CUT:

5 10½" strips. Sub cut into **20** 10½" squares.

Note: If fussy cutting, a 10½" ruler will make the job easier.

FROM THE ACCENT FABRIC 1, CUT:

12 2½" strips. Sub cut into **20** 14½" strips, and **20** 10½" strips.

FROM THE ACCENT FABRIC 2, CUT:

12 2½" strips. Sub cut into **20** 14½" x 40" strips, and **20** 10½" x 40" strips.

FROM THE INNER BORDER, CUT:

6 2½" strips.

FROM THE OUTER BORDER, CUT:

7 8½" strips.

FROM THE BINDING, CUT:

8 2¼" strips.

Piecing the Blocks

1 Divide the big-print fabric squares into two piles, 10 in each pile. Half the blocks will be framed with accent fabric #1 and half with accent fabric #2.

2 Working with a square from one pile, add a 10½ strip of accent fabric #1 to the top and bottom as shown in Figure 1. Press toward the accent fabric. Add a 14½" strip of accent fabric #1 to each side as shown. Press toward the accent fabric.

3 Set the 12½" square-up ruler on top of a block. Turn the ruler to the left until the corners of the ruler touch the outside edges of the framing fabric as shown in Figure 1. Trim. This is Unit A, make 10.

JOIN STRIPS TO THE TOP AND BOTTOM.

JOIN STRIPS TO THE SIDES.

ROTATE SQUARE-UP RULER AND TRIM.

Fig. 1. Unit A. Make 10.

4 Add a 10½" strip of accent fabric #2 to the sides of a big-print square from the remaining pile. Press toward the accent fabric. Add a 14½" strip of accent fabric #2 to the top and bottom. Press toward the accent fabric.

5 Set the 12½" square-up ruler on top of a block. Turn the ruler to the right until the corners of the ruler touch the outside edges of the framing fabric as shown in Figure 2. Trim. This is Unit B, make 10.

JOIN STRIPS TO THE SIDES.

JOIN STRIPS TO THE TOP AND BOTTOM.

ROTATE SQUARE-UP RULER AND TRIM.

Fig. 2. Unit B. Make 10.

Assembling the Top

1   To make Row Y, join two A Units and two B Units as shown in Figure 3. Press seams toward accent fabric #1. Make 3.

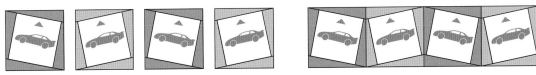

Fig. 3. Row Y. Make 3.

2   To make Row Z, join two B Units and two A Units as shown in Figure 4. Press seams toward accent fabric #1. Make 2.

Fig. 4. Row Z. Make 2.

3   Join Rows Y and Z as shown in Figure 5. Press.

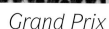

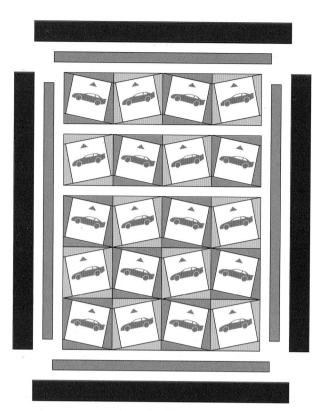

Assembly Diagram

Adding the Borders

1 Join the strips for the inner border together by sewing diagonal seams. Press open. Join all of the strips together until you have one long strip.

2 Measure the length of the quilt lengthwise *through the middle.* This will prevent you from having wavy borders. Mathematically this number would be 60½", but everyone's seam allowances vary, so be sure to measure. Cut two strips the length of your quilt. Attach one to each side of the quilt. Press.

3 Now measure the quilt crosswise *through the middle.* This measurement should be approximately 52½", but check your measurement to be sure. Cut two strips this length. Add them to the top and bottom of your quilt. Press.

4 Repeat Steps 1–3 with the outer border fabric.

Finishing Your Quilt

1 Cut your backing fabric into two equal pieces. Remove selvages. Sew the long sides of the backing pieces together.

2 Prepare your quilt sandwich following the Layering and Basting instructions on page 12.

3 If you have gone to the trouble of fussy cutting the big-print fabric for this quilt, you'll want to be sure that the quilting doesn't detract from the image. This can be accomplished by outlining the designs or echo quilting around them.

4 Bind and label your quilt following the instructions on page 13.

See page 9 for an example of this design featuring a T-shirt block.

Frame-Up Table Runner

A beautiful Asian print will add grace and charm to any table.

Pieced and quilted by Connie Nason.

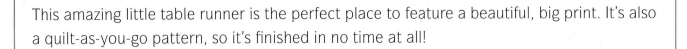

This amazing little table runner is the perfect place to feature a beautiful, big print. It's also a quilt-as-you-go pattern, so it's finished in no time at all!

Measurements

Runner: 15" x 48"

Fabric Requirements

- 1½ yd. big-print fabric
- ½ yd. inner border
- ⅓ yd. outer border
- 18" x 52" batting

Choosing Fabric

While my friend Connie was piecing this in my studio, we came up with all kinds of great possibilities for table runners—holidays, retro kitchen, seasonal, even something special for the "kid's table" at family get-togethers. While there is enough fabric for the front and back of this runner, you could choose to use something different for the back and make it reversible. *Consider making this quilt using the following type of fabrics: scattered prints, packed prints, directional prints or novelty prints. You could also use this design to showcase appliqué blocks.*

Cutting Instructions

Note: All strips are cut across the width of the fabric.

FROM THE BIG-PRINT FABRIC, CUT:

Cut along the fold of the fabric. Set half aside to use for the backing. From the remaining piece, cut a 9½" x 42" rectangle, fussy cutting if desired. Fold the rectangle into quarters. Lay the 45-degree line of a ruler along the cut edge of the fabric and trim to a point.

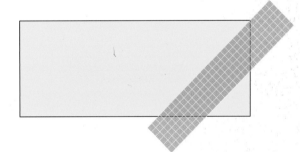

Fig. 1. Making the point.

FROM THE INNER BORDER AND BINDING, CUT:

3   1½" strips.
3   2¼" strips.

FROM THE OUTER BORDER, CUT:

3   2½" strips.

FROM THE BACKING, CUT:

1   18" x 52" strip.

Piecing the Runner

1 Pin or spray baste the batting to the wrong side of the backing. Center the big-print fabric on the batting, right sides up. Pin.

> *Note: A walking foot can make stitching through several layers much easier.*

2 Lay an inner border strip along one long side of the big-print fabric with right sides together. Stitch through all layers. Trim the excess fabric; there should be some excess fabric at both ends. Press open. Repeat on the other long side as shown in Figure 2.

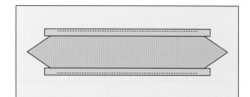

Fig. 2.

3 Trim the excess fabric so it is flush with the angled sides of the big-print fabric as shown in Figure 3.

> *Note: To accurately cut the inner border strips, fold the ends so the fold is flush with the angled side of the big print. Slip a pair of scissors into the fold and trim.*

Fig. 3.

4 Repeat Steps 2 and 3 with the remaining inner border strips as shown in Figure 4. After joining the strips and pressing open, trim the ends so they are flush.

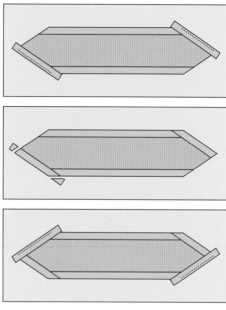

Fig. 4.

5 Repeat Steps 1–4 above with the outer border fabric as shown in Figure 5.

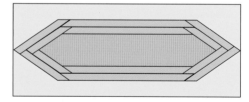

Fig. 5.

6 To make the binding, join the binding strips together with diagonal seams. Add the binding strips to runner before trimming. Once the binding has been stitched down, trim the runner and finish the binding as usual.

7 Add additional quilting around the motifs in the big print fabric.

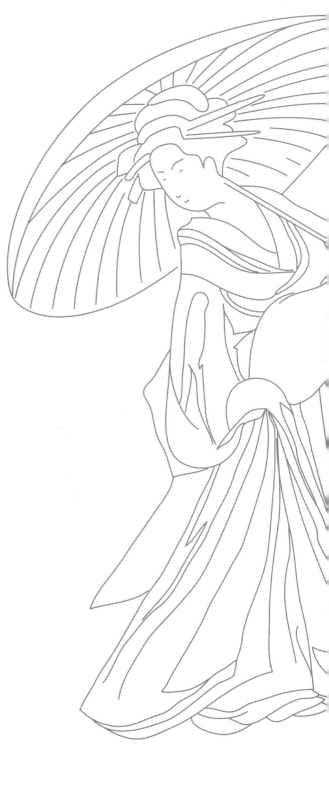

Grand Canyon

The subtle contrast of the big-print fabric and accent fabric give this quilt a soft, blended effect.

Pieced by Connie Nason and quilted by the author.

Windmills were a common site on farms and ranches across America. The wind generated power was used to draw water up from the ground. It's no wonder that the common windmill found its way into our foremother's quilts. Now, when driving across the county, I love to see the power generating windmills running along ridges in stately rows. The windmills in this pattern remind me of that, all neatly lined up. There's plenty of room in between them to show off a pretty print!

Measurements

Quilt: 81" x 98"
Block: 12"

Fabric Requirements

- 6¼ yd. big-print fabric
- 3 yd. accent fabric
- 5⅔ yd. backing
- 85" x 102" batting

Choosing Fabric

The sample quilt here has a very soft, blended feel but this is a pattern that you could take in a completely different direction. Choosing a pinwheel fabric with more contrast would really make the design pop. *Consider making this quilt using the following type of fabrics: packed prints or novelty prints. You could also showcase embroidered blocks, appliqué blocks, photo transfers or sampler blocks.*

Cutting Instructions

Note: All strips are cut across the width of the fabric.
Note: For ease of construction, used the Gridded Triangle Method on page 15.

FROM THE BIG-PRINT FABRIC, CUT:

3   15" strips for gridded triangles. Sub cut into **11** 15" x 9" rectangles.*

4   12½" strips. Sub cut into **12** 12½" squares.

6   4½" strips. Sub cut into **48** 4½" squares.

2   7" strips. Sub cut into **11** 7" squares. Cut each square twice diagonally for small side setting triangles.

1   3¾" strip. Sub cut into **2** 3¾" squares. Cut each square once diagonally for small corner triangles.

8   2½" strips for inner border.

9   6½" strips for outer border.

FROM THE ACCENT FABRIC, CUT:

3   15" strips. Sub cut into **11** 15" x 9" rectangles.*

8   4½" strips for middle border.

8   2¼" strips for binding.

* If not using the Gridded Triangle Method, cut **12** 2⅞" strips. Sub cut into **164** 2⅞" squares.

Piecing the Blocks

PINWHEELS

1 See page 15 for instructions on Gridded Triangle Method. Make 328 half-square triangles.

Fig. 1. Half-square triangles. Make 328.

2 To make a Pinwheel block, join four half-square triangles together. Press toward the accent fabric.

Fig. 2. Pinwheel Square. Make 82.

WINDMILL BLOCKS

1 Lay out five Pinwheel blocks (each corner and center) and four 4½" squares of big print fabric.

2 Join the block together in rows. Press toward the big print fabric.

Fig. 3. Join blocks together

3 Join the rows together to make the Windmill Block. Make 6.

Fig. 4. Windmill Block. Make 6.

SIDE SETTING BLOCK A

1   Lay out four Pinwheel blocks, two 4½"
    squares of big print fabric and three small
    side setting triangles.

2   Join the blocks together in rows. Press
    toward the focus fabric.

Fig. 5. Side Setting Block A.

3   Join the rows together to make a Side
    Setting Block A. Make 6.

SIDE SETTING BLOCK B

1   Lay out four Pinwheel blocks, two 4½"
    squares of big print fabric, four small side
    setting triangles and one small corner
    triangle.

2   Join the blocks together into rows. Press
    toward the focus fabric.

Fig. 6. Side Setting Block B.

3   Join the rows together to Side Setting
    Block B. Make 4.

CORNER SETTING BLOCK A

1 Lay out three Pinwheel blocks, one 4½" square of big print fabric, four small side setting triangles and one small corner triangle.

2 Join the blocks together in rows. Press toward the focus fabric.

Fig. 7. Corner Setting Block A.

3 Join the rows together to make a Corner Setting block A. Make 2.

CORNER SETTING BLOCK B

1 Lay out three Pinwheel blocks, one 4½" square of big print fabric, two small side setting triangles and one small corner triangle.

2 Join the blocks together into rows. Press toward the focus fabric.

Fig. 8. Corner Setting Block B.

3 Join the rows together to make a Corner Setting Block B. Make 2.

Assembling the Top

1 Working on a design wall or on the floor, lay out the pieced blocks, and 12½" square of big print fabric as shown in the Assembly Diagram.

2 Join the blocks together in diagonal rows.

3 Press the seams toward the big print fabric. This will allow the seams in each row to nest with the seams in the row next to it.

4 Join the rows together diagonally. Press.

Assembly Diagram

Adding the Borders

1 Join the strips for the inner border together by sewing diagonal seams. Press open. Join all of the strips together until you have one long strip.

2 Measure the length of the quilt lengthwise *through the middle.* This will prevent you from having wavy borders. Mathematically this number would be 74" but everyone's seam allowances vary, so be sure to measure. Cut two strips the length of the quilt. Attach one to each side of the quilt. Press.

3 Now measure the quilt crosswise *through the middle.* This measurement should be approximately 61" but check your measurement to be sure. Cut two strips this length. Add them to the top and bottom of your quilt. Press.

4 Repeat Steps 1–3 with your middle border fabric, then outer border fabric.

Finishing Your Quilt

1 Cut your backing fabric into two equal pieces. Remove selvages and join together.

2 Prepare your quilt sandwich following the Layering and Basting instructions on page 12.

3 This quilt would be a good candidate for quilting only in the big-print fabric and leaving the pinwheels unquilted. If a small stipple is used in the big-print fabric, the pinwheels would stand out from the background. For a quick finish, I chose to do twisting ribbons on this quilt. I thought they helped carry out the feeling of things blowing in the wind.

4 Bind and label your quilt following the instructions on page 13.

Big Bertha

The large and medium scale floral prints in this quilt share the same colors, creating an overall blended look.

Pieced and quilted by the author.

This quilt is not only stunning to look at, it's very simple to piece. Strip sets eliminate piecing together lots of little squares. Bands of diagonal blocks create movement and interest on the surface of the quilt.

Measurements

Quilt: 76" x 96"
Block: 10"

Fabric Requirements

- 4¼ yd. big-print fabric
- 2 yd. medium scale floral
- 1½ yd. red
- 1 yd. green
- ⅔ yd. print for inner border
- 5⅝ yd. backing
- 80" x 100" batting

Choosing Fabric

If using floral prints, you need to find a large scale and medium scale print that have the same colors throughout, or at least the same color in the background. This will insure that the blocks blend together and allow the diagonal squares to become the main design focus in the quilt. If you have a large scale floral that you truly love, but can't find another to match it, you could repeat it in place of the medium scale fabric. Depending on how strong you want the diagonal element to be, choose fabrics with little contrast or distinct contrast for the accent squares. Repeating the large scale floral for the outer border is a good choice. *Consider making this quilt using the following type of fabric: packed prints. You could also showcase embroidered blocks, appliqué blocks, photo transfers or T-shirt blocks.*

Cutting Instructions

Note: All strips are cut across the width of the fabric.

FROM THE BIG-PRINT FABRIC, CUT:

5 10½" strips. Sub cut into **17** 10½" squares.

6 5½" strips. Sub cut into **10** 10½" x 5½" rectangles and **4** 15½" x 5½" rectangles.

9 6½" strips for the border.

FROM THE MEDIUM FLORAL, CUT:

3 1½" strips.
3 6½" strips.
16 2½" strips.

FROM THE RED FABRIC, CUT:

2 1½" strips.
11 2½" strips.
9 2¼" strips for binding.

FROM THE GREEN FABRIC, CUT:

2 1½" strips.
11 2½" strips.

FROM THE INNER BORDER, CUT:

8 2½" strips.

Piecing the Strip Sets

Note: *There are five different blocks that make up the body of the quilt. Strip piecing certain units will make assembling the blocks easier.*

STRIP SET A

1 Join a 1½" red strip with a 1½" green strip. Press toward the green. Repeat to make a second strip set.

2 Cut into forty-six 1½" two-patch segments. Set 10 segments aside.

3 Join remaining segments to make 18 four-patches 18 four-patch blocks.

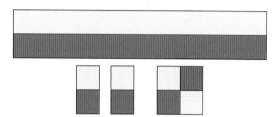

Fig. 1. Strip Set A. Two- and Four-Patches.

STRIP SET B

1 Cut one 2½" square from the end of six 2½" green strips, six 2½" red strips and nine 2½" medium floral strips. Set aside. These will be used in Strip Set D & E.

2 Use the remaining strips from Step 1 to make 3 Strip Set B.

3 Cut into forty-two 2½" segments.

Fig. 2. Strip Set B. Make 3. Cut into 42 segments.

STRIP SET C

1 Join a red and green 2½" strip to each side of a medium floral 6½" strip to make Strip Set 3. Make 3.

2 Cut into forty-two 2½" segments.

STRIP SET D-RED AND STRIP SET D-GREEN

1 From a 2½" medium floral strip, cut four 8½" rectangles.

2 Join a red 2½" square to one end of a rectangle. Strip Set D-Red. Make 2.

3 Join a green 2½" square to one end of a rectangle. Strip Set D-Green. Make 2.

Fig. 4. Strip Set D. Make 2 of each color.

Fig. 3. Strip Set C. Make 3. Cut into 42.

STRIP SET E-RED AND STRIP SET E-GREEN

1 From a 2½" medium floral strip, cut four 6½" rectangles.

2 Join a red 2½" square and a floral 2½" square to one end of a rectangle. Strip Set E-Red. Make 2.

3 Join a green 2½" square and a floral 2½" square to one end of a rectangle. Strip Set E-Green. Make 2.

Fig. 5. Strip Set E. Make 2 of each color.

STRIP SET F

1 From three 1½" strips of medium floral, cut twenty 4½" rectangles.

2 Add a rectangle to each side of a red/green two-patch. Make 10.

Fig. 6. Strip Set F. Make 10.

STRIP SET G

1 From five 2½" floral strips, cut thirty-six 4½" rectangles.

2 Add a rectangle to each side of a four patch. Check for orientation of the four-patch, being sure the red patch is in the upper left corner. Make 18.

Fig. 7. Strip Set G. Make 18.

Piecing the Blocks

1 Join a Strip Set F to a Strip Set B, and a Strip Set C. Note the orientation of the Green squares, as shown in Fig. 8. Press. Make 4.

Fig. 8. Make 4.

2 Join a Strip Set F to a Strip Set B, and a Strip Set C. Note the orientation of the Red Squares, as shown in Fig. 9. Press. Make 6.

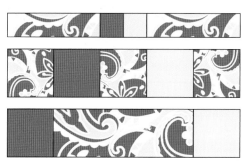

Fig. 9. Make 6.

3 Join a Strip Set D-Green, Strip Set E-Green, Strip Set G, Strip Set B, and Strip Set C. Note the orientation of the Green squares, a shown in Fig. 10. Press. Make 2.

Fig. 10. Make 2.

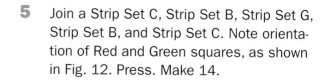

4 Join Strip Set D-Red, Strip Set E-Red, Strip Set G, Strip Set B, and Strip Set C. Note the orientation of the Red squares, as shown in Fig. 11. Press. Make 2.

Fig. 11. Make 2.

5 Join a Strip Set C, Strip Set B, Strip Set G, Strip Set B, and Strip Set C. Note orientation of Red and Green squares, as shown in Fig. 12. Press. Make 14.

Fig. 12. Make 14.

Assembling the Top

1 Working on a design wall, or on the floor, lay out the blocks and big print fabrics as shown the Assembly Diagram on page 101. Check the orientation of the diagonal lines of color.

2 Join the blocks together in rows.

3 Press the seams toward the large floral blocks. This will allow the seams in each row to nest with the seams row below it.

4 Join the rows together, starting at the top of the quilt. Press.

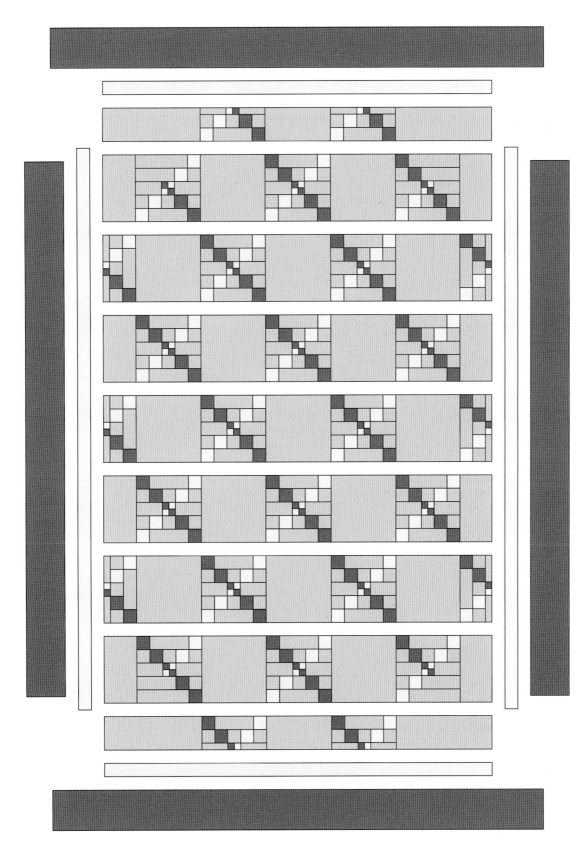

Assembly Diagram

Adding the Borders

1. Join the strips for the inner border together by sewing diagonal seams. Press. Join all of the strips together until you have one long strip.

2. Measure the length of the quilt lengthwise *through the middle.* This will prevent you from having wavy borders. Mathematically this number would be 80½", but everyone's seam allowances vary, so be sure to measure. Cut two strips the length of the quilt. Attach one to each side of the quilt. Press.

3. Now measure the quilt crosswise *through the middle.* This measurement should be approximately 64½", but check the measurement to be sure. Cut two strips this length. Add them to the top and bottom of your quilt. Press.

4. Repeat Steps 1–3 with your outer border fabric.

Finishing Your Quilt

1. Cut the backing fabric into two equal pieces. Remove selvages and join together.

2. Prepare your quilt sandwich following the Layering and Basting instructions on page 12.

3. Because of the scale and business of the fabric, this quilt was quilted with a rather large stipple. Any fancy stitching would be wasted on a quilt like this, as the stitches will disappear into the design of the fabric. However, the stipple did not go through the red and green squares, allowing them to stand out from the rest of the design.

4. Bind and label the quilt following the instructions on page 13.

See page 9 for an example of this design featuring an appliqué block.

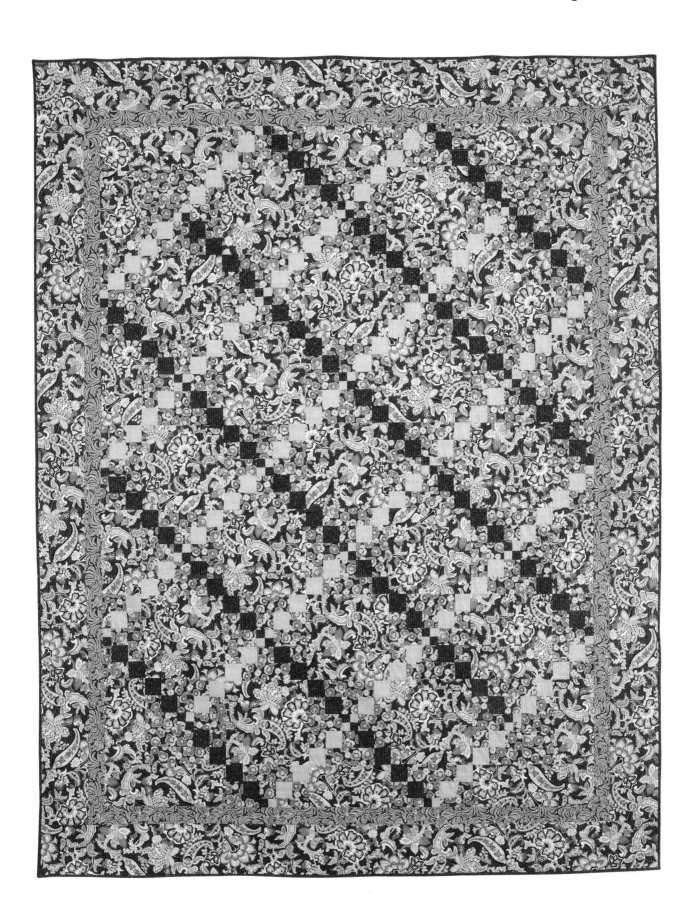

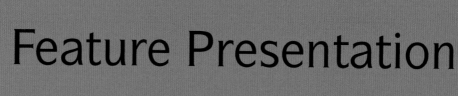

Feature Presentation

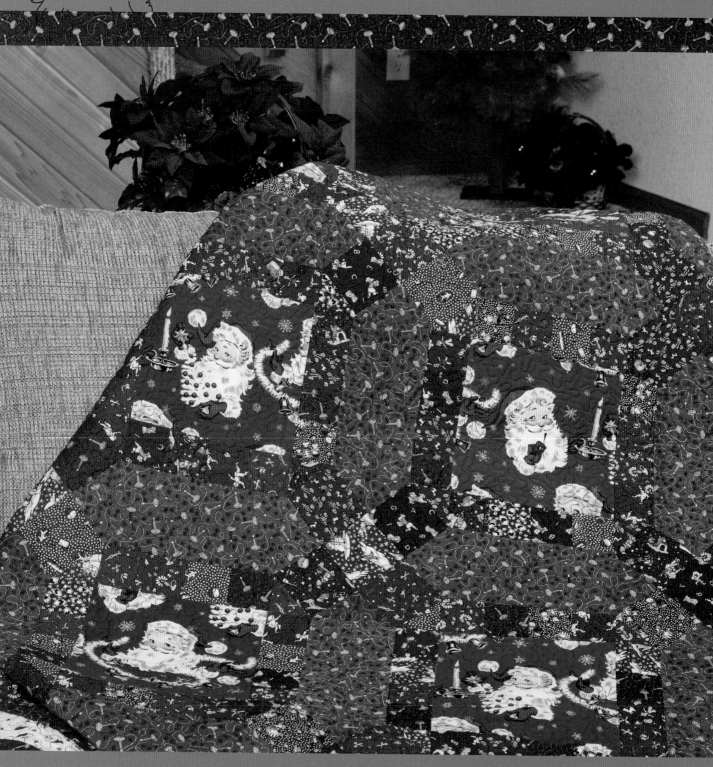

This holiday quilt has an air of nostalgia.

Pieced and quilted by the author.

Beverly Wakeman taught a traditional Garden Maze quilt class at my shop. She had given her quilt a unique spin by using a black background and Amish solids for her quilt. However, I had a small piece of vintage Christmas fabric that I really wanted to feature in a holiday quilt. When I spied the six large squares in this design, I knew I'd found the right vehicle to make it happen.

Measurements

Quilt: 52" x 68" (68" x 84")
Block: 8"

Fabric Requirements

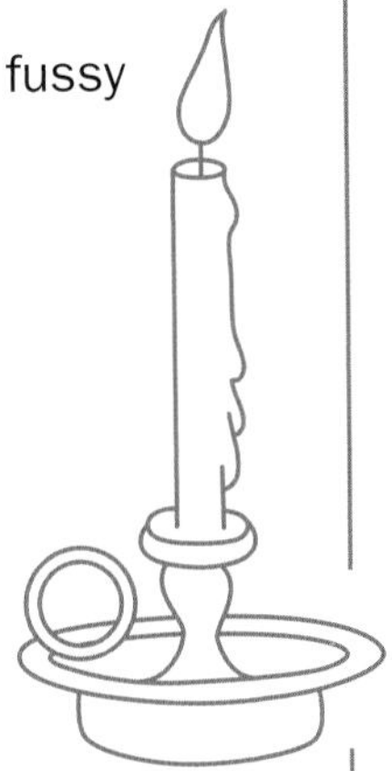

- ⅝ (⅞) yd. big-print fabric—more if fussy cutting
- 1¼ (1⅝) yd. green background
- 1⅝ (2½) yd. assorted reds
- ⅜ (1½) yd. white inner border
- ¾ (1) yd. red outer border
- ⅝ (⅔) yd. green binding
- 3¼ (5) yd. backing

Choosing Fabric

There are two things to keep in mind when choosing fabrics for this quilt. First, in order to achieve the effect of the garden maze, you will want the background fabric to match the background of your big-print fabric. Second, the assorted prints should not only be the same color, but the same value. A large assortment of prints will result in a more interesting quilt. In the sample, most of the reds have a Christmas theme, but not all of them. I chose reds that had the same value, rather than just a Yuletide theme.

Value is the intensity of color, not the color itself. You can purchase a value finder to help you determine the value of your fabrics. When you look at fabrics through this little red lens, it takes away the color and lets you see if some of the fabrics are lighter or darker than others.

Consider making this quilt using the following type of fabrics: scattered prints, directional prints or novelty prints. You could also showcase embroidered blocks, appliqué blocks, photo transfers or T-shirt blocks.

Cutting Instructions

Note: *All strips are cut across the width of the fabric.*
Note: *Numbers in ( ) represent instructions for the larger 68" x 84" size quilt..*

FROM THE BIG-PRINT FABRIC, CUT:

2 (3) — 8½" strips. Sub cut into **6 (12)** 8½" squares.

FROM THE GREEN BACKGROUND FABRIC, CUT:

5 (8) — 4½" strips. Sub cut into **17 (31)** 4½" x 8½" rectangles.

2 (3) — 5¼" strips. Sub cut into **12 (20)** 5¼" x 5¼" squares. Cut each square in half twice diagonally.

1 (1) — 4" strip. Sub cut into **4 (4)** 4" squares.

FROM THE ASSORTED REDS, CUT:

60 (100) — 3⅜" squares.
136 (248) — 2½" squares.
24 (40) — 2⅞" squares. Cut each square in half once diagonally.

FROM THE WHITE INNER BORDER, CUT:

5 (7) — 2" strips.

FROM THE RED OUTER BORDER, CUT:

6 (8) — 4" strips.

FROM THE GREEN BINDING, CUT:

7 (9) — 2¼" strips.

Piecing the Blocks

Note: *There are three different blocks that make the design in this quilt.*

BLOCK A

1   Join 3 different 3⅜" red squares into a strip. Add a red 2⅞" triangle to each end of the strip. Make 12 (20).

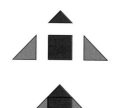

Fig. 1. Unit X. Make 12 (20).

2   Join a green quarter square triangle to each side of a 3⅜" red square. Join a red 2⅞" triangle to the top as shown in Figure 2. Make 24 (40).

Fig. 2. Unit Y. Make 24 (40).

3   To make Block A, join a Unit Y to both sides of a Unit X as shown in Figure 3. Make 12 (20).

Fig. 3. Block A. Make 12 (20).

BLOCK B

1   Join 4 different 2½" red squares into a strip as shown in Figure 4. Make 34 (62).

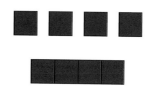

Fig. 4. Unit Z. Make 34 (62).

2   To make Block B, add a Unit Z to each side of a 4½" x 8½" green rectangle as shown in Figure 5. Make 17 (34).

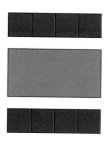

Fig. 5. Block B. Make 17 (34).

BLOCK C

Block C is the 8½" square of big-print fabric.

Assembling the Top

1 Working on a design wall or on the floor, lay out the blocks as shown in the Assembly Diagram.

2 Join blocks together in rows. Press.

3 Join the rows together. Press.

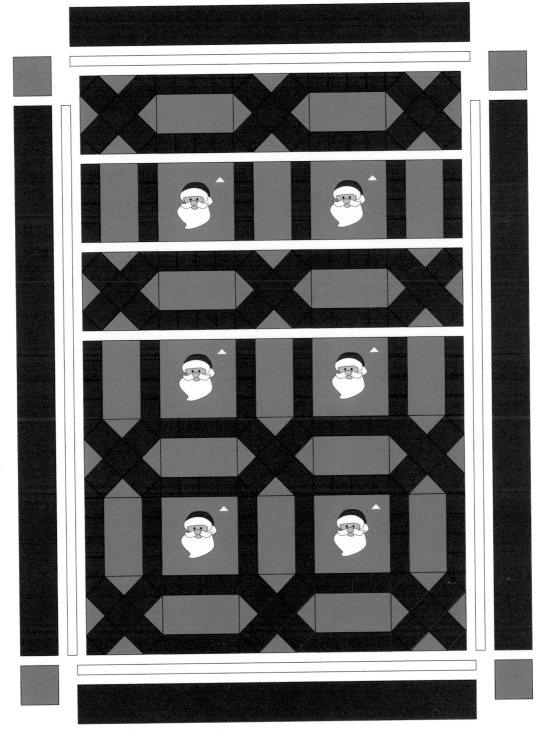

Assembly Diagram

Adding the Borders

INNER BORDER

1 Join the strips for the inner border together by sewing diagonal seams. Press open. Join all of the strips together until you have one long strip.

2 Measure the length of the quilt lengthwise *through the middle.* This will prevent you from having wavy borders. Mathematically this number would be 56½" (72½") but everyone's seam allowances vary, so be sure to measure. Cut two strips the length of the quilt. Attach one to each side of the quilt. Press.

3 Now measure the quilt crosswise *through the middle.* This measurement should be approximately 43½" (59½"), but check your measurement to be sure. Cut two strips this length. Add them to the top and bottom of the quilt. Press.

OUTER BORDER

1 Join the strips for the outer border together by sewing diagonal seams. Press open. Join all of the strips together until you have one long strip.

2 Measure the length of the quilt top lengthwise *through the middle.* This will prevent you from having wavy borders. Mathematically this number would be 59½" (75½") but everyone's seam allowances vary, so be sure to measure.

3 Before adding borders to the sides of the quilt, measure your top crosswise *through the middle.* This measurement should be 43½" (59½") but check your measurement to be sure. Cut two strips this length. Add a 4" green square to each end of these strips.

4 Attach borders from Step 2 to each side of the quilt. Press. Attach borders from Step 3 to the top and the bottom of the quilt. Press.

Finishing Your Quilt

1 Cut the backing fabric into two equal pieces. Remove selvages and join together.

2 Prepare your quilt sandwich following the Layering and Basting instructions on page 12.

3 Because the Santa quilt used lots of busy prints, I chose to finish it with an all over stipple. If I had used calmer fabrics in the borders, they would have been a good place to do some special quilting.

4 Bind and label your quilt following the instructions on page 13.

Resources

Andover Fabrics, Inc.
1384 Broadway, Suite 1500
New York, NY 10018
(212) 710-1000
800-223-5678
www.andoverfabrics.com

Anna Lena's Quilt Shop
PO Box 1399
111 Bolstad Avenue
Long Beach, WA 98631
(360) 642-8585
www.annalena.com

Annie's Attic
1 Annie Lane
Big Sandy, TX 75755
(800) 582-6643
www.anniesattic.com

Keepsake Quilting
Route 25
P.O. Box 1618
Center Harbor, NH 03226-1618
(800) 438-5464
www.keepsakequilting.com

Krause Publications
(888) 457-2873
www.krause.com

About the Author

Big Print Quilts is Karen Snyder's forth book. It follows the popular *Bundles of Fun* and *Fat Quarter Fun*, and her new book *Quilts from My Garden*. Besides designing quilts and authoring books, Karen owns Anna Lena's Quilt Shop and designs 1930s reproduction fabrics—called Wash Tub Prints—for Andover Fabrics.

Although she always knew that she would someday be a quilter, Karen didn't start quilting until 1995 when she received a free quilt pattern in the mail. Once she started hand piecing that Grandmother's Flower Garden, she was hooked and hasn't looked back.

Make the Most of Big Prints and Bold Colors in Your Quiltmaking

FAT QUARTER FUN
by Karen Snyder

Indulge in the guilty pleasure of fat quarter quilts and you'll be glad you did, with 150 step-by-step photos, and 15+ projects, you'll find countless ways to have bundles of fun.

Softcover · 8¼ x 10⅞ · 128 pages
75 b&w illus. · 150 color photos
Item# Z0934 · $22.99

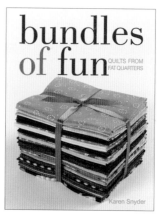

BUNDLES OF FUN
Quilts From Fat Quarters
by Karen Snyder

Explore advice about fabric selection, instructions for making smaller quilts and adding sashing and borders in this book, and use what you learn to create variations for 12 coordinating projects.

Softcover · 8¼ x 10⅞ · 128 pages
150+ color photos and illus.
Item# FQLQ · $22.99

QUILTS FROM MY GARDEN
20 Projects with Recipes Fresh from the Garden
by Karen Snyder

Do your gardening indoors with 20 beautiful sewing and quilting projects and 10 delicious recipes, all inspired by your garden. Collection of recipes and projects in this guide are perfect for any skill level.

Softcover · 8¼ x 10⅞ · 128 pages
50 color photos
Item# Z1320 · $22.99

CALIENTE QUILTS
Create Breathtaking Quilts Using Bold Colored Fabrics
by Priscilla Bianchi

Learn five methods for mixing and matching exotic fabrics from around the world for a fresh approach to contemporary quilts, while you explore the 120+ radiant photos of quilts and fabrics in this guide.

Softcover · 8¼ x 10⅞ · 144 pages
200+ color photos and illus.
Item# Z0103 · $24.99

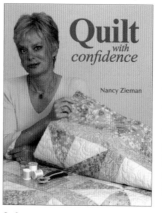

QUILT WITH CONFIDENCE
by Nancy Zieman

Leading sewing expert Nancy Zieman covers topics including tool selection, organizing the quilting area, rotary techniques, seaming and much more to give beginning quilters the confidence they need to keep quilting.

Softcover · 8¼ x 10⅞ · 144 pages
100 color photos
Item# Z1549 · $24.99